Creative Followership

Second book of Creative Followership Series

Jimmy's Stories

Creative Followership

Second book of Creative Followership Series

Jimmy's Stories

Preaching What I Practiced at Chick-fil-A®

Jimmy Collins with Michael Cooley

Creative
Followership™

Published by Looking Glass Books, Inc. Decatur, Georgia

Distributed by John F. Blair, Publisher, Winston-Salem, North Carolina

Quantity sales at discounts are available to nonprofit organizations, schools, and associations. Contact Creative Followership, LLC, www.creativefollowership.com

Creative Followership is a trademark of Creative Followership, LLC.
Chick-fil-A, a registered trademark of CFA Properties, Inc., is used with permission.

Printed in the United States of America.

Cover design: Irene Morris Design
Book design and composition: Burtch Hunter Design

All scripture quotations are taken from the New American Standard Bible (Lockman Foundation 1995). Used by permission.

Cover photo: Veer AYP1272919

Library of Congress Cataloging-in-Publication Data:
Names: Collins, James L. S., 1936- author. | Cooley, Michael R., author.
Title: Jimmy's stories : preaching what I practiced at Chick-fil-A / by Jimmy Collins, with Michael R. Cooley.
Description: Decatur, Georgia : Looking Glass Books, Inc., [2015] | Series: Second book in creative followership series
Identifiers: LCCN 2016005171 (print) | ISBN 9781929619665 ()
Subjects: LCSH: Leadership. | Followership. | Collins, James L. S., 1936- | Chick-Fil-A Corporation.
Classification: LCC HD57.7 .C64533 2015 (print) | DDC 650.1--dc23
LC record available at http://lccn.loc.gov/2016005171

First Edition

*I dedicate this work to all of you who have so often
encouraged me to tell a story.*

J.C.

All of the stories in this book are from my real-life experiences.
They are all true. Where appropriate, names have been changed
to protect individual privacy.

All of my references to anything that occurred while I was an
employee of Chick-fil-A, Inc., are based on my memory of the
events. My memory may vary from that of others. Statements
about or involving Chick-fil-A policies, business practices,
and legal issues are not intended to comply with correct legal
terminology or current or past business policy or practices.

Chick-fil-A, Inc., has not approved this book or authorized me
to speak on its behalf.

He who tends the fig tree will eat its fruit,
And he who cares for his master will be honored.

KING SOLOMON (PROVERBS 27:18)

Contents

Contents

M ost of us have a desire to accomplish something bigger than we can accomplish alone. When we followers are drawn to a leader with an attractive vision, a unifying purpose, there is no limit to what we can accomplish together.

It is the leader's unifying purpose that attracts the interest and loyalty of followers. The leader is someone who is able to communicate the unifying purpose in a manner that is inspiring, persuasive, or motivating. The unifying purpose joins the followers to the leader.

The Creative Followership logo illustrates the three essential components of leadership, followership, and unifying purpose. The large arrow represents the unifying purpose. The small arrows represent the leader and followers, held together by the unifying purpose. The leader is in the center of the unifying purpose, out front, leading the followers. The followers have joined the leader and are supporting him or her in fulfilling the unifying purpose.

ACKNOWLEDGMENTS

Even though I have stories that I want to tell, I don't like to write and I don't write very well. Michael Cooley is my firsthand, always available helper. Just knowing that he will review, often rewrite, and be the first editor of my work improves my performance.

Having stories does not make a book. That is why I relied on Dick Parker at Looking Glass Books to help make these stories into a book, then to distribute and get it to market. As before, he was there to help make the vision a reality.

Whatever Michael and I missed or messed up, Todd Manza set right. Todd not only knows how to say and spell the words correctly, he has an eye for consistency and balance that I highly value. It is hard for me to appreciate how much I need him until he finishes his edit. Then I know!

A book is something to hold in your hand and read. After the words are right, they still need to be displayed in an attractive and easy-to-read manner. Burtch Hunter is the magician that took the stories and made the book.

Attractive wrapping on a package motivates us to open it. And Irene Morris knows how to make a beautiful wrapper for a book. Not only did she give us an attractive wrapper, but also her design told its own story of what a reader can expect upon opening the book. It clearly invites the reader to sit and read a story.

I am thankful for all that these folks did to help produce the second book in the Creative Followership series. I hope you enjoy the stories.

—Jimmy Collins

INTRODUCTION

Preaching What I Practiced at Chick-fil-A

I preach what I practiced.

As a boy, and long before I recognized how dramatically they shaped my life, I enjoyed reading and listening to stories. Whether it was about the Little Engine That Could, saying, "I think I can, I think I can" as he pulled his train up the mountain, or about the boy David, with his slingshot aimed at the giant Goliath, the narratives both captivated my imagination and firmly embedded in my mind their timeless principles.

Would I have so eagerly learned and retained the moral without the story? There is no doubt about it: without the vehicle of the story, I would never have remembered any of these principles.

As I grew older, I gradually became more acutely aware of the priceless value of stories to enhance my memory. Tell me a story that clearly describes a point or principle that you want me to remember and I will definitely remember it.

If stories are so valuable for my own recollection of what I hear or read, it must also be so for others. Even though I am a slow learner, I got the message after a while: if I teach and present to people by using stories, they will remember the principles.

If you want people to remember what you say, tell stories.

When I present Creative Followership to an audience, I tell them, "I know that you will not remember much of what I say. To help you remember my main points and the principles of Creative Followership, I will tell you stories. All of my stories are true."

This book is a collection of my stories.

The stories are true. The characters are real people I know personally. I have occasionally changed the names, to protect the privacy of individuals, but the events and situations are real. I did not create or combine different events or times to make a better story.

During my thirty-two years at Chick-fil-A, stories were an essential part of how I communicated. I employed all of these stories many times over the course of my career, and in speaking engagements since that time.

I used stories in my conversations, correspondence, presentations, and reports to staff and Operators (franchisees) because people can't put into practice procedures or policies that they can't remember.

Most of these stories have appeared on my website, **creativefollowership.com**. A few are also in my book *Creative Followership: In the Shadow of Greatness*. I'm sure some will find a home in books I will write in the future.

A good story is worth repeating, and I believe these are some of my best. I hope you enjoy them.

—Jimmy Collins

You will not remember much of what I say.
To help you remember, I will tell stories.
All of my stories are true.

Jimmy's Stories

Tell Your Own Story

On a Sunday afternoon in the autumn of 1946, after a fried chicken dinner, all of the men—my daddy, my uncles, and my older cousins—gathered on the back porch of Grandma's old and weatherworn sharecroppers' house. Those who were too late to get one of the rocking chairs just brought a cane-bottom straight chair from the house and leaned back against the wall. We boys sat anywhere we could find a space, waiting for the real feast to begin.

It was storytelling time! The war was over, but nothing would ever be the same again, except the wonderful stories the men shared. As soon as one storyteller finished, another stepped forward with an even better story along the same line. The longer it went on, the more memorable the stories. It fascinated me that every man had his own story on every subject, usually confirming the objective of the previous man's story.

While listening to the stories, I visualized myself as the main character of each story. I was the one who tamed that stubborn mule. That was me, walking five miles through the snowstorm to rescue the puppy. There I was, driving the tractor that the landlord bought last month. These stories were mine!

Slowly, the foggy curtain of unknowing was pulled away and I learned a lesson of a lifetime.

Good storytellers have their own version of the story.

A valuable lesson, but more was to come. When I was about 25, searching for the secrets to enhancing my career, I attended a two-day leadership training seminar featuring a long list of highly rated professional speakers on leadership, motivation, salesmanship, and self-development. On the second day, a man went to the microphone and used an elaborate story to illustrate his point. It was a good story, well delivered, but another speaker had told that same story the previous day.

That's not all. Before the seminar was over, I heard several jokes told more than once. I don't know if I was more surprised or disappointed to hear much of the material repeated by others who spoke later. Had I expected too much by believing that every speaker would have unique material?

Now the second part of the lesson was also coming into view.

Good speakers and writers use original material.

This is a principle that I practice and advocate.

Tell your own story.

I package my own stories, in my own original material. When I am introduced, the audience is expecting to hear from me—not my teachers, not my boss, not a historical figure, but from me.

I will not disappoint you or them, or embarrass myself, by using someone else's stories or material.

How about you?

Stories to Remember

Why do you tell those stories about when you were young?

That's a question I am glad to answer. When I write or speak, I want to do more than just reach those who read or hear my message. I want them to remember my main point or points.

Seldom are many people in the audience interested in the facts or details; they just want to know what, if anything, is worth remembering, the main points. As you are fully aware, most of what is written and said is not worth remembering. So, the audience usually is not expecting or prepared to remember very much, if anything.

My message of Creative Followership is directed primarily to an audience that ranges from young adults to middle-aged folks. I want to get their attention, be certain that I get the message into their minds, and see that it stays there. To do that, I try to package my main points in simple, true stories from my own experience.

Think about it: what has every living adult experienced? Whether we are young, middle age, or seniors, we all recall those wonderful days of our youth. Yes, there were some bad days, but forget them. What is remembered are the wonderful days. To get my points registered in an audience's memory, my objective is to have each person in the audience picture him- or herself as the main character in my story. If I can get that image in their mind, they will definitely remember the main points of the message for a long time.

That works because people do not remember what I say; they remember what they think about while I am speaking.

They will remember because it's no longer me *telling* the story; it is them *living* the story. It becomes their story.

When you read or hear my story, don't you think of a similar situation from your life? Of course you do. The details won't be the same, the setting will be different, but the outcome will have just as much impact. You will not only be reading or hearing; you will be living a virtual experience.

The younger I can paint the picture of the main character in my story or illustration, the greater is the number of people in the audience who will virtually live the role of the main character. My goal is to take the entire audience with me.

This practice works for me. Why don't you try it?

Tell stories about when you were young.

That will give more people the opportunity to live, virtually, the role of the main character in your stories.

What Every Leader Must Have

There are leaders and there are followers. This is not a complex idea. As a matter of fact, and by definition, there are no leaders *unless* there are followers.

A leader is someone who has followers.

There is no need to add adjectives to the word *leader* to explain various styles of behavior or levels of performance. A leader is someone whom another person has chosen to follow. It is simple. A leader is someone who has followers.

A follower is someone who has chosen a leader.

A follower is a volunteer. You cannot hire, bribe, coerce, force, or enslave someone to follow a leader. That would certainly not be a leader/follower relationship. It is simple. A follower is someone who has chosen a leader.

What would cause someone to follow another person? What would cause you to follow another person?

For a leader/follower relationship to form, there must be something that draws them together. Then there must be something that keeps them together.

Some observers would have us believe that a leader attracts followers through charm, intelligence, personality, or persuasiveness, yet there are multiple examples in which this does not explain why the follower is attracted to the leader.

After the follower connects with the leader, what is it that holds them together? Everyone knows that leaders and followers stick together during bad times as well as good. Often, we see the bond strengthened by leaders and followers weathering the worst and most difficult situations together. So what is this powerful force that attracts and holds followers to the leader?

Every leader must have a unifying purpose.

The unifying purpose is the basis of the relationship between the leader and the follower.

The unifying purpose is the magnet that attracts followers to the leader. The leader has a purpose that he or she is able to communicate clearly and simply. That purpose is a magnetic force that attracts followers. The followers see an opportunity to join the leader for the accomplishment of a worthy purpose. The followers choose a leader with a unifying purpose, a purpose that they want to help the leader accomplish. The leader's purpose then becomes the follower's purpose, which makes it their unifying purpose.

Then, as leader and followers work together to accomplish the unifying purpose, that purpose becomes the glue that holds them together. The leader constantly communicates and defines the purpose, while the followers create the organization and execute the purpose. They are bound together during good times and bad because they share a joint desire to accomplish their unifying purpose. For all of them, it is no longer the leader's purpose; it is "our purpose."

Without the unifying purpose, there is no leader, and there is no follower.

The unifying purpose joins leader and follower together.

The Viewpoint of
the Follower

Why are there so few books on the practice of followership?

The authors of the best books that I have read on followership have based their message on research or observation. Reading their books is helpful if you are interested in studying followership as subject matter. However, someone interested in the actual *practice* of followership would find it more helpful to understand followership from the viewpoint of the follower. There is no substitute for the experience of a person who has actually practiced followership.

My book *Creative Followership: In the Shadow of Greatness* is about the practice of followership. Creative Followership, as I advocate it, is presented from the viewpoint of the follower.

Every employee has many relationships that affect his or her career. As an employee, you must be able to satisfy the organization's customers or clients, maintain a good working relationship with your coworkers, and of course, please your boss.

Absolutely, the most important relationship for any employee is with the boss. That is why I place so much emphasis on choosing your boss, knowing your boss, making your boss successful, and pleasing your boss.

I use stories of my own experiences to illustrate how Creative Followership worked for me. Creative Followership was my pathway to success and satisfaction in my thirty-two-year career at Chick-fil-A. I know that what worked for me will work for anyone, at any level of responsibility, in any organization. My purpose is to motivate and inspire others to adapt, in their own careers, what worked for me.

My mission is to share Creative Followership with those who need it most and to help them understand how much it can enhance their careers. I want readers to see that this is a better way to approach their careers, and to learn to use it to achieve the success and satisfaction they desire.

Are you just beginning your career journey?

Would you like to restart your career on a better pathway?

Are you ready for more responsibility?

Would you like to have a better relationship with your boss?

If you answered yes, the practice of Creative Followership is for you!

First Job, First Day

First job, first day. What a learning experience that was for me, for you, for everyone.

I needed a job—a job with a steady income. I worked for people in the neighborhood, cutting grass and raking leaves, but the work was unpredictable and didn't provide the steady income I needed. My parents provided my basic necessities, but it was up to me to earn my own money for nonessentials.

Finally, John Brown hired me.

The year was 1948; I was 12 years old. The world was different then. It was not unusual for a 12-year-old to have a part-time job after school and on Saturdays. This was especially true in the lower-middle-income neighborhood where my father, my mother, and their five children lived.

Neighborhood grocery stores were important because many people did not have an automobile. Some folks walked to the store to buy groceries; others called to place orders by telephone. Most customers without automobiles appreciated the store's free delivery service.

My job was to deliver the groceries on a bicycle for John Brown's grocery store. The cycle truck had a large wire basket above the small front wheel, and a large rear wheel. In addition to delivering groceries, I was to do whatever chores Mr. Brown assigned to me.

The first day, I discovered why Mr. Brown had hired me! He had hired me to do what he did not like to do.

He did not like to dust the shelves, sweep the floor, fill the soft drink cooler, write the prices on the cans and boxes, keep the merchandise tidy, wash the windows, clean up spills, or carry out the trash.

Mr. Brown certainly did not like delivering groceries on that bicycle!

Did I mention that Mr. Brown did not own an automobile?

As the day progressed, I realized, *If I do what the boss does not like to do, Mr. Brown will keep me on this job and I will be able to earn a steady income.*

I had discovered one of the key principles of Creative Followership on the first day of my first job.

Do what your boss does not like to do.

When I did what the boss did not like to do, I added value to his business. It gave him more time to do the things he liked to do, the things that only he could do, the things that added higher value than I could contribute. When I did what he did not like to do, he wanted me to be there and he knew that I was worth what he paid me.

On every job since that day in 1948, I have practiced this principle of Creative Followership. It has earned me

A Genuinely Daunting Day!

my boss's support and the respect of my coworkers every-where I have worked.

I recommend it because it has been tested and has proven worthy. It worked for me. It will work for everyone.

It will work for you.

If you want to enhance your career,

Do what your boss does not like to do.

Choose Your Boss

Have you ever thought about looking for a boss rather than looking for a job?

Think about it. If you work within an organization, you probably have a boss. Within an organization, you *need* a boss.

Yes! I did say, "You need a boss."

You need someone to function as an icebreaker to clear the path ahead. You need someone who knows the way and can smooth the path for you as you journey toward your objectives of success and satisfaction. You need someone with those important contacts both within and outside the organization. You need a coach and a teacher. Certainly, you need someone to praise you in the hearing of those in the best position to recognize and reward your outstanding performance.

Yes! You really do need a boss.

When you consider how important your boss is to your future within the organization, you will see why I advise you to

Choose your boss.

This is Creative Followership Principle 1. But it must

be done carefully. If you work for the wrong boss, you risk your career. You only have one life. Don't waste it working for the wrong boss. If you have the wrong boss, fire that boss and choose another—in reverse order, of course.

If you choose the right boss and help him or her advance through the organization, you will ride that same train. The right boss will recognize and appreciate your contributions, will see to it that you receive appropriate credit and compensation, and will take you where you want to go.

Choose your boss.

Ride the Right Train

At daybreak on April 19, 1969, my wife, Oleta, and I boarded the Central of Georgia Railway's deluxe passenger train, the Nancy Hanks II, from Savannah to Atlanta. We looked forward both to the ride and to the excellent food service on this train. Breakfast was served between Savannah and Macon, and lunch was served between Macon and the grand old Terminal Station in Atlanta.

We planned to enjoy a relaxed journey home after the super busy grand opening week of Chick-fil-A of Oglethorpe Mall, the second Chick-fil-A mall restaurant. We chose the train so that we could spend time together, dreaming and planning our future.

During that train ride, Oleta and I recognized our many opportunities and counted them as blessings. Our spirits were soaring, and all doubts were rapidly fading into obscurity.

When we boarded the Nancy Hanks II, we were in for a six-hour, two-hundred-mile ride. I tell young people, "When you choose the right boss, you can ride his or her train for a long way." It is in that sense that I am describing the "train" my family climbed aboard five months before the grand opening at Oglethorpe Mall, when I decided that Truett Cathy was the right boss for me. When we boarded Truett's train, we were on board for a thirty-two-year, multimillion-mile ride.

The beginning of our journey with Chick-fil-A went smoothly. A lease in the new enclosed Oglethorpe Mall came quickly. As a matter of fact, the developer, Scott Hudgens, sought us out. His wife, a Chick-fil-A fan, shopped at Greenbriar Mall in Atlanta and told him that he should get Truett to open a Chick-fil-A restaurant in his new Oglethorpe Mall.

In fact, everything had worked out reasonably crisis-free when we opened this second Chick-fil-A mall location. We had no problems obtaining permits and licenses. We had hired a building superintendent and built the leasehold improvements ourselves.

On the day of the grand opening, the people of Savannah flooded the beautiful new mall and freely spent their money there. Opening sales at the new restaurant were excellent.

As Truett would often ask later, "Is everybody happy?" By our smiles and actions, we all replied, "Yeah, man, H-A-P-P-Y!"

Getting locations would never be that easy again. Until we had a solid market position with outstanding sales, opening restaurants in enclosed malls presented significant challenges. Mall developers were not interested in having quick-service restaurants in their brand-new malls. We faced enormous difficulties in securing permits and

Nancy Hanks II

licenses, dealing with contractors, negotiating with unions, and trying to work with government regulators. These obstacles tested us to the limit.

When I look back, I am glad we didn't give a second thought to the challenges and difficulties ahead. I am glad we didn't know how difficult it would be to build a restaurant chain.

That knowledge would not have discouraged me, but it certainly would have detracted from the joyful feeling of accomplishment and adventure that surrounded Oleta and me on the train ride home that day.

We were on Truett Cathy's Chick-fil-A train, and we were going to ride, ride, and ride.

Success, make ready. Here we come!

Common Sense and Creative Followership

I received this e-mail from a reader of my book *Creative Followership: In the Shadow of Greatness.*

"Jimmy, there is nothing unique about your book. It is just plain old common sense."

My reply: "Yes, but how many young people know it?"

His response: "Not many!"

There seems to be a prevailing attitude that only the rare and expensive things in life are valuable.

Is a secret more valuable than information that is easily available? Do you have to earn an MBA or PhD in order to learn what is important for you to achieve success and satisfaction in your career? Is commonly known information less valuable than the less-known bits of information?

What do you think?

Old folks believe that common sense or commonly known principles and practices are more valuable than anything we can acquire from formal education. If you don't believe me, just ask them.

Why do they put high value on the readily available knowledge that they like to call common sense? They know the value of common sense because of their real-life experiences. Experience has proven what works!

Whether or not you share old folks' feeling about common sense, you will at least have to admit that, unequivocally, they believe in it and live it!

So, is Creative Followership just plain old common sense?

Some people have told me that Creative Followership is counterintuitive. What does that mean?

Could it be true that we failed to rise above the "I am only interested in me" era of a few years ago?

Yes, the practice of Creative Followership does require that we help the boss succeed, cooperate with our fellow workers, and satisfy customers. This means that, to succeed, we must accept a role in which we give priority to the needs of others in order to fulfill our own needs.

Is that common sense? You decide!

As for me, I am casting my vote with the old folks!

Followership... A Tiny Niche?

As an unpublished author, I was searching for a literary agent to help me convince a first-rate publisher that I had a book that potential readers would willingly purchase.

Even if you have not tried it yourself, you have heard the stories about how difficult it is to find a publisher.

One literary agent who replied to my letter wrote, "Jimmy, you need to rewrite your book as a leadership book. Followership books do not sell. You have written for a tiny niche."

Have I written for a tiny niche? I don't think so.

Over the last thirty-two years of my career, I was a follower of Truett Cathy, the founder of Chick-fil-A. When I joined Truett, there was one freestanding Chick-fil-A restaurant and one small restaurant in an enclosed mall shopping center. When I retired, the sales from our more than nine hundred restaurants exceeded $1 billion a year. Today, fourteen years later, the Chick-fil-A restaurant chain is even larger.

There are 1,200 Chick-fil-A restaurant Operators (franchisees); these Operators—the word is always capitalized, as a sign of respect—are the *leaders*. They have more than 70,000 employees; these employees are their *followers*.

Look at the numbers and ask yourself, are followers a small niche? Not in my experience!

I have written for the largest audience: the followers!

I know some of you are wondering, What about the employees who are team leaders, rising leaders, and so on?

My answer is that all of them are followers. Anyone who is following someone else is a follower. Even most of the people we refer to as leaders are actually followers. In fact, when we examine all of the relationships, it is very difficult to identify many people who are not followers of someone.

There seems to be a fear of being identified or classified as a follower, but why are so few people willing to be identified as followers? Maybe it is fear of being lost and unnoticed among the vast number of followers, or maybe it is simply fear of the unknown.

Here is why you should not be afraid to be a follower and should consider practicing Creative Followership.

When I decided to abandon the pursuit of authority and leadership roles, I discovered a new and refreshing freedom to advance my career. I call it Creative Followership.

As a creative follower, I decided to take responsibility for the difficult, dirty, and high-risk tasks, those that no one else wanted. Because I was willing to take responsibility, the risk of failure was exclusively mine. Once I took full responsibility for failure, however, my coworkers did not hesitate to join with me. I had removed the risk for them but had left open the path to a share of the credit for success.

The practice of Creative Followership was not only a more open and less crowded pathway to success and satisfaction; it became a magnet that attracted many people to cooperate with me. People wanted to work with me.

When I was participating in the struggle for leadership roles, titles, and authority, I was *competing* with them. When I became a creative follower, my coworkers no longer viewed me as a competitor.

The whole world of my career changed. Because I was no longer competing with my coworkers, they were cheerfully joining me, in a spirit of cooperation.

I had gone from an atmosphere of *competition* to one of *cooperation*. As a result, I found there was no limit to what I could accomplish.

Choosing the path of Creative Followership led to a satisfying career for me. I used it at every level of responsibility.

The field is wide open. There are no secrets to discover and no rules to follow. Anyone can be a creative follower.

Join me in the practice of Creative Followership. It will work for anyone, at any level of responsibility, in any organization.

It will work for you!

Do You Feel Underpaid?

How many times have you felt underpaid? What did you do about it?

Most people that I have discussed this issue with respond in the same way. They tend to say things like:

"I feel underpaid."

"I am convinced that my boss does not appreciate me."

"I am discouraged. I will do what I need to get by, but I am definitely not going to do any more."

"I will let my boss know I am discouraged, by refusing to do anything extra that he wants from me."

"I will show my boss that if she wants more from me, she will have do more for me first. That should teach her to treat me right!"

Sound familiar? Been there? Done that?

That kind of mind-set will result in an ever-descending, downward-spiraling boss/worker relationship. You lose. Your boss loses. Most regrettable of all, the boss is not likely to ever figure out what happened.

Interested in learning a better approach?

Do more than is expected.

It worked for me, and it will work for you. Here is how

I used this Creative Followership principle.

I have never felt overpaid, though I have many times felt grossly *under*paid. At the same time, I realized that it did not matter to the boss how I felt. What mattered was how my boss felt!

I had to make my *boss* feel that I was underpaid.

A good way to get the boss to feel that he is underpaying you is to constantly do more than the boss expects. Do it sooner than expected. Do it better than expected. Do what you know the boss wants done *before* she asks or tells you. Do the things the boss does not like to do. Do it the way the boss likes it done.

By using this principle, you can convince your boss that he or she is underpaying you. The objective, in fact, is to make your boss feel embarrassed that he or she is so grossly underpaying you!

You can feel underpaid forever and never get a raise, or you can make your boss feel you are underpaid and get the raise you deserve.

This almost always works. However, if you have a boss who is so out of touch that he cannot see how valuable you are, or you work for someone so cruel that she is not willing to pay you fairly, fire your boss. Of course, it is best to find a new boss first, one who will appreciate just how valuable you are.

It is good to feel underpaid—if you also make your boss feel that you are underpaid.

Do more than is expected!

Getting the Wrong Results?

Do you see the similarity between the following two incidents?

I had just checked into my favorite motel in Johnson City, Tennessee, and had asked for my usual extended checkout time. The desk clerk's response shocked me.

"I can't do it anymore," she said. "The home office has cut my labor budget and eliminated all overtime. I can't have a maid stay past her normal quitting time."

I never returned to that motel.

Our family was on our way south to Florida, on I-75, and it was time to stop for lunch. We took the next exit for a quick meal at a major chain hamburger restaurant. The service was slow, with an especially long wait for french fries. My family carried the rest of the food to the table and sat down while I stayed at the counter and waited . . . and waited . . . and waited.

This incident occurred years ago, when the chain had first added drive-thru service. I could see that orders placed after mine, from the drive-thru, were being filled first. When I brought this to the attention of the manager, she said, "I have to send food to the drive-thru customers first because the home office is tracking serving times on the drive-thru." When I asked, "What about us dining room customers?," her reply was, "Well, they are not tracking that."

It is not difficult to understand why customers feel that drive-thru service is faster than the service inside.

Do you see what is happening in both incidents?

Someone with considerable authority is measuring the wrong thing. There is a difference between knowing how to count and knowing what is most important to measure. Unfortunately, this happens far too often. No doubt, you can recall many incidents where you have seen this same situation.

Whatever you measure, be sure that it accurately reflects what is important to know. Otherwise, you gather interesting numbers that actually confuse or deceive, and that distort important decisions.

Be careful!

Measure the wrong thing and you get the wrong results.

And getting the wrong results can lead to making the wrong decisions!

Avoid this mistake and you will enhance your career and protect your reputation.

Learn from Bad Bosses

D o you work for a bad boss? If so, I have good news: you can learn from bad bosses.

You may not like your bad boss. You may want to fire your bad boss. You may already be looking to replace your bad boss with a good boss. Despite all of this, you can be learning some valuable lessons from that bad boss.

It is not even necessary for that bad boss to be *your* boss. You can also learn from someone else's bad boss. I learned many good lessons from other people's bad bosses.

When I was 16 years old, I learned from my father's bad boss. My father was a receiving clerk in a warehouse for a large tire manufacturer.

My younger brothers and I wanted Daddy to go somewhere with us after work one day. As usual, he had ridden the bus to work that morning. We called him and told him what we wanted, and he said, "Drive the car and come pick me up when I get off from work. I will ask my boss if I can leave a few minutes early."

When we arrived at the warehouse, about thirty minutes before the end of the workday, I heard my father ask his boss, "I have finished my work and my boys are here to pick me up. May I leave a few minutes early?"

The boss's surly reply was, "I don't care if you finished early. You'll leave when I tell you to, and not one minute early."

We all stood there and waited for the workday to end so Daddy could clock out.

When we got in the car and left, we all discussed the incident in detail. It was obvious to us boys that the boss wanted us to know that he was in charge and that he intended to make Daddy look inferior in our presence.

We were distressed that our father tolerated such an abusive boss. Even though we realized that Daddy had very little formal education, we didn't think he should have to put up with the behavior of that boss. One of my brothers said he should have given the boss a bloody nose.

After hearing our opinions, Daddy said, "Boys we have to learn to accept people as they are. We may not like the way they behave, but we can't change them. Besides that, a man needs a job."

I learned two valuable lessons that day.

First, I resolved that, if I ever found myself in authority over anyone else, I would not treat him or her the way that bad boss had treated my father.

Second, I realized that although Daddy's abusive boss may have intended to portray my father as spineless and unmanly, he had failed. What my brothers and I saw was a strong man who cared so much for his family that he could, without showing resentment, tolerate that bad boss without yielding his pride and confidence. Never before had it been so clear how much my father loved me. I wanted to be more like Daddy.

To me, personally, the second lesson was priceless. However, that takes nothing away from the importance of the first lesson. Today, more than sixty years later, my vivid memory of that afternoon is still guiding my thinking and behavior.

Learn from bad bosses.

You can learn from bad bosses, even someone else's bad boss. Bad bosses provide valuable life lessons you will always remember.

The First Principle
of Time Management

When the end of the day rolls around, have you ever thought to yourself, *Where did my time go today?*

If so, do you often vow to manage your time better tomorrow? Do you commit to doing a better job of planning?

Most people do. Their intention is good. But the action taken is hopeless.

In *The Effective Executive* (1967), Peter Drucker writes, *Effective executives . . . do not start out with planning. They start by finding out where their time actually goes.*

In 1965, when I began my practice of commercial kitchen design consulting, I recognized that the sum total of what I had to sell was my time. It was essential that I make maximum use of my time. When I looked around to see which of my friends did the best job of managing their time, my accountant and lawyer friends appeared to be doing the best job. They tracked and sold their time.

From the beginning of my consulting practice, therefore, I tracked my time.

I had discovered the most important principle of time management: know where your time goes.

Know where your time goes.

While working as a consultant, I tracked my time in fifteen-minute increments. Obviously, when I sold my services by the hour, I had to know how much time I used in order to bill my client. For negotiated price commissions, too, it was essential to know where the time went, to determine whether I had calculated an accurate time required to do the job. Having this information assured me that I could sell my services with the confidence that I would not lose money on a project.

The next year, Drucker's *Effective Executive* confirmed my time-tracking approach: *The effective executive therefore knows that to manage his time, he first has to know where it actually goes.*

Later, when I went to work for Truett Cathy at Chick-fil-A, I continued to track my time. Periodically, I would analyze how I spent my time on a monthly and quarterly basis. That actual time-use information was what I needed to make more effective use of my time.

I knew where my time was going.

Too many people base their time management solely on how they *intend* to spend their time. But I found that managing my time by referring to what had been scheduled on a calendar was next to worthless! How many days actually happen as you plan?

As the years passed and my responsibilities increased, I began to track my time expenditure in five-minute increments. I tracked everything, including trips to the coffee break room or restroom, walk-around time, personal phone calls—you name it, I tracked it.

Time tracking is not nearly as time consuming as you might think. I kept my Day Runner open on my desk, showing all of my planned time use for the day, and simply made a note whenever I changed what I was doing. It was simple, easy, and quickly done.

You need to know that I am an expert time waster. If I had not tracked my time, I would have accomplished very little. If you don't also track the time you waste, you will never know how much more you could do simply by eliminating some of that waste.

Again, Peter Drucker agrees: *Time is the scarcest resource, and unless it is managed, nothing else can be managed.*

Do you want to get more done?

Know where your time goes.

This worked for me, and it will work for you!

Are you willing to try it?

Know where your time goes.

My Way or the Highway

There is a popular expression of power that often is used when referring to the attitude of a tough boss. Some of those bosses enjoy stating it themselves. I have worked for more than one boss who liked to say, "It's my way or the highway!"

During my twenties, I worked for three different food service equipment dealers. At one company, I had a boss who appeared to favor two men whom I was confident I was outperforming.

I was baffled.

In sales, I consistently ranked with the top performers. Even though I was one of the youngest salespeople, I was the only one capable of designing, selling, and installing the equipment for a complete food service operation. In fact, I had designed kitchens for more of the local high-name-visibility restaurants than anyone at any of the food service equipment dealers in our market area.

Nonetheless, confrontations with my boss were a regular occurrence. It seemed that I seldom pleased him, no matter how productive my performance.

If my conflict with the boss was not due to my performance, it had to be something else. I thought maybe it was related to lifestyle, because mine was very different from that of the two men he favored, but I could not see any substantial similarity in the lifestyle of those two men. In fact, their backgrounds could not have been more different: one was aristocratic and sophisticated, the other was redneck and rough.

The boss was not like either of them. He was competent, socially active, and respected in the local business community. None of us three salesmen had, at that time, the same type of connections the boss had—actually, none of us traveled in the same circles at all. All four of us had a different lifestyle, so whatever caused the boss to favor the other two men must not have been a lifestyle issue.

Why did I not receive the favor and recognition that accrued to the other two men?

Then, one day it dawned on me. How could I have been so blind for so long?

Those other two men did everything exactly the way the boss liked it done!

I had rediscovered another principle of Creative Followership. Even though I had known this principle, I had not been actively using it, and not using it had cost me my boss's favor and had handicapped my advancement within the company.

Do it the way the boss likes it done.

As I began to apply this principle and do it the way the

boss liked it done, my status with my boss improved amazingly!

Unfortunately, this boss and I had some fundamental differences in our ethics and attitudes about how people should be treated and business should be conducted. He asked his employees to do things that I was not willing to do. I knew that to be successful in my relationship with my boss, I must be willing to do it the way the boss liked it done. In this situation, though, there were too many times when I could not do that.

My choice? Do it the way the boss likes it done or choose a new boss.

I decided that "My way or the highway" was not a slogan exclusive to bosses. I used it myself. I fired my boss and took to the highway.

Of course, I did choose a new boss before I fired the one I was leaving.

Do it the way the boss likes it done.

Do New Brogans Leak?

It was early September 1942. I prepared to enter the first grade at Church Street Elementary School. My mother had made me shirts and bought new denim overalls. Getting ready for school also required a lunch box, a raincoat, and a new pair of shoes.

Mother took me to Buster Brown in downtown Atlanta for the new shoes. She selected a pair of brown leather, high-top, lace-up brogans with rubber soles and heels. They were miniature versions of the shoes all of the men in my family wore while working in the cotton fields.

I was proud of those shoes. One new pair of shoes per year was the limit in my nonwealthy family. None of us children wore shoes in the summer.

I remember the first day that it rained after I got those new shoes. Some of the kids had been teasing me, saying I was wearing "farmworker" shoes to school. Most of the boys wore high-top Keds sneakers. I wanted to prove to my friends, once and for all, that my brogans were much better than their sneakers. I knew that I could win the argument; sneakers were not as good as brogans because sneakers would leak but brogans were waterproof. The first rainy

day gave me the opportunity I was looking for to conduct a test that would prove my brogans were leakproof.

During the half-mile walk home from school, I stepped in every puddle of water I found. Even though I didn't know it at the time, that day I invented a principle of Creative Followership:

Never assume what you can verify.

I wanted to be certain my shoes did not leak. They did not.

To say that my mother was not interested in me inventing principles of Creative Followership would be a gross understatement.

Nonetheless, the practice of this principle saved my reputation many times during my career. There were hundreds of times when my boss, Truett, asked me, "Are you sure?" I always wanted to be prepared to say, "Yes!"

Nothing makes you look as foolish, careless, and unprepared as advocating a position or action that you could have verified, but chose not to, and that turns out to be dead wrong. If you can verify something, do it.

There are many situations in which information is vague or nonexistent and can't be verified, but always verify when verification is possible.

Never assume what you can verify.

The practice of this principle will enhance your career and protect your reputation.

Learn to Say No

The word *no* might be the most important word in the English language.

Proper use of this word will signal to the world around you who you really are.

It can clearly communicate what you believe, what you stand for, the value you place on your integrity, and the limit of your courage.

When it is properly used, you do not have to write it in bold letters or italics or underline it. When you say it in a conversation, you do not have to shout it aggressively or feel like you need a bullhorn to announce it. Just a soft, firm no will work just fine, if it is sincerely and assertively stated.

Learn to say no.

This two-letter word can be the most useful in a creative follower's toolbox of words.

It can prevent you from losing your integrity. Saying no can keep you from deviating from the unifying purpose. You can protect your boss from embarrassment. It can secure your role as a valuable follower. There are people who have a gift for making people say yes rather than no, and a creative follower must be on guard in the presence of those who make it hard to say no.

If you are not willing or not able to say no when negotiating to buy or sell an automobile, a horse, or real estate, you will never make the best possible deal—and you could get stuck with a really bad one. If the wrong person proposed marriage to you, would you say no? Of course you would!

But what would you do if your boss asked you to tell a lie? Would you be able to say no in the very same way? You can and you should be able to say it, quickly and assertively, in both cases.

While I was working as a restaurant equipment salesman, I negotiated a cost-plus contract to furnish all the equipment for a new restaurant. The buyer was a good-natured, easygoing man whom my boss perceived to be very trusting and naive. The boss told me not to let the buyer know the full extent of the discounts we received from the manufacturers, because the buyer should not know our real cost.

This was my reply: "I will not lie *to* you and I will not lie *for* you." The subject was never brought up again.

Learning how and when to say no is essential for confident assertiveness and responsible decision making.

Learn to say no.

That Is Not in
My Job Description

Mary is a woman who changes jobs often. As a result, it is not unusual for her to have long periods of unemployment between jobs.

Several months ago, she told me that she had a new job she was pleased with, and that she liked her boss. She was bubbling over with excitement, because she had been unemployed for many months.

Last week, when I asked her about her new job, she replied, "I quit that job."

"What happened?" I asked.

She said, "That boss wanted me to do things that were not in my job description. It was not what she hired me to do, and she was not paying me to do more than what was in my job description."

Mary is no longer young and, unfortunately, has never learned an important principle of Creative Followership. She has read my book, has a pleasant personality, is honest and trustworthy, and is a good worker, but she is not willing to practice this principle.

Do more than is expected.

How about you? Are you willing to do more than is

expected—whether because the boss asks or without being told?

You will probably be able to keep your job by meeting the minimum expectations in your job description. But if you do only the required minimum, you are not likely to be rewarded with pay increases or promotions, even if the boss keeps you.

Think about Mary's situation. Maybe Mary's new boss wanted to see whether Mary was capable of the work involved in a higher-paying position. Maybe her boss wanted to see how Mary reacted to a more stressful role or to more responsibility. Mary may have missed a track that would have led to more responsibility and a higher-paying job.

If you want to advance your career, you will need to do more than the minimum. That means you must do more than is expected. When the boss asks you to do more than is in your job description, seize that opportunity to show what you can do. When you recognize that something needs to be done, do it before the boss has to ask.

To advance your career, you must make the boss glad that you are on his or her team. Convince the boss that not only do you want more responsibility but also you can handle it. Remember, you want to convince your boss that you are worth more than you are currently being paid!

To receive the recognition and reward that we all desire, you must

Do more than is expected.

Select the Right People

It was Chick-fil-A's annual Operators Seminar. Fred arrived for his requested private meeting with the CEO, Truett Cathy, and me.

Fred was a very dissatisfied Operator. He had operated his restaurant for seven months and was struggling. Sales—and thus his income—were not meeting his expectation. He was on the verge of giving up.

When Truett asked for Fred's evaluation of the problem, Fred responded with a long list of negatives: his mall was not fully leased, there were not enough shoppers, the mall owner was not advertising enough, the stores in the mall did not appeal to the local shoppers—he went on and on.

That is, he would have gone on, if Truett had not stopped Fred when he said, "It is a terrible labor market. I can't get any good employees."

Truett said, "Tell me about your employees."

Fred said, "That's probably my worst problem. I can't get good employees. My turnover rate is out of sight. Before I can get them trained, they leave. But they are so bad, I am glad to see them go. I wish they would all leave."

Truett asked, "Who selected those employees?" Then he just sat there, looking at Fred, for a long time.

Eventually, Truett broke the very long silence with this advice: "Select the right people and you will eliminate most of your problems."

You have seen it; I have seen it; everyone has seen it: employees can make or break a business. In fact, as Peter Drucker puts it in *The Frontiers of Management* (1986), *Of all the decisions an executive makes, none are as important as the decisions about people.*

Fred accepted Truett's advice. He went back to his restaurant and invested his time and energy in making good people decisions. As a result, his sales soared and so did his income.

As a creative follower, your responsibilities will grow and expand. You will be involved in people decisions. Remember that your most important decisions will be people decisions—who does what—and these start with *who*.

You must select the best person first, then assign the best person for the task to be done. That is, *who* . . . does . . . *what.*

I am a realist. I know you can't make a silk purse out of a sow's ear. You have to hire people to fit the job, while also remembering that God does not make people to fit job descriptions. There are no perfect fits. You have to select the best *available.*

When selecting people, the four most important components are:

45

1. character,
2. personality,
3. knowledge, and
4. skills.

You can impart knowledge and teach skills, but you cannot change character or personality.

Do I need to say more?

Select the right people and you will eliminate most of your problems.

That's what worked for me.

Fire Your Boss

Would you like to fire your boss?

If you said yes, then what are you waiting for?

Sometimes people work for the wrong boss, year after year, and complain that they are going nowhere within the organization. Why do they do it?

Probably the number one reason is fear of the unknown. They are afraid to go out and look for a new boss. They may be reluctant to look around because they do not know how their employer will react if he or she finds out they are looking.

Looking for a new boss does require discretion, and some courage. On the other hand, think of what you have to lose if you continue to stay right where you are, with the wrong boss.

Another excuse I frequently hear is, "I don't like my boss, but I do like the organization." It is essential to realize that, even in good organizations, there are likely be bad bosses, go-nowhere bosses, and incompetent bosses. Often, the better alternative to looking outside your current organization is to look for a transfer to a good boss of your choice within the same organization. Workers with good performance records and friendly personalities usually don't find it difficult to get a transfer. In most organizations, bosses are constantly on the lookout for up-and-coming workers they can add to their staffs.

It is your future. Why not take control and direct your career where you want it to go? If you are not satisfied with your boss, don't just sit there and complain; do something about it.

Choose a new boss and fire your current boss.

Fire your boss.

My First Date

Do you remember your first date? I do! It is no exaggeration to say it was a memorable event.

Unlike most of my friends, I went on my first date at a rather young age. I asked a girl, Sarah, to go out with me when I was 9 years old. We were both in the third grade at Church Street Elementary School in East Point, Georgia. I asked her to go to a movie with me after school, and she said yes. At that point, I was on an emotional high. Everything was great, and the world was a wonderful place for Sarah and me!

My real-world education was about to begin.

It started when my father said, "You can't go alone." That made no sense to me. Every Saturday, I went to the movies alone, or with other kids from the neighborhood. I always went without an adult chaperone. It got worse. He said, "I don't mean an adult chaperone. You can take Tommy." Tommy is my little brother. Daddy said, "Take him or you don't go." I took him.

This story doesn't get better. On the morning of the date, it was raining. We didn't have a car, so we walked everywhere, and my mother insisted that Tommy and I

Jimmy standing on left end of fourth row

wear our raincoats and galoshes to school. In those days (1945–46), Church Street Elementary had no cafeteria. Everyone carried lunch to school. I asked to carry our lunch in a paper bag, so we could throw the bag in the trash after lunch, but Mama insisted that we use those nice, metal lunch boxes, because they would keep our lunch from getting wet on the way to school.

Picture this, if you can. School has let out for the day. The rain stopped long ago. The sun is shining. And here we are, two boys, ages 9 and 7, wearing galoshes over our shoes, carrying raincoats and lunch boxes, each with an armload of schoolbooks, arriving at Sarah's house. Yes, we left all of that stuff on her front porch.

Sarah and I walked to the movie theater, with Tommy tagging along behind. She and I sat together and shared popcorn. After the movie, we walked back to her house.

Tommy and I picked up our stuff and went home.

The outcome of that blown adventure was that I decided that the pleasure of dating was just not worth the hassle and potential embarrassment of unexpected complications. I was discouraged.

It was seven years later before I went on my second date. This time, the girl asked me, and the outcome was totally different. When I returned home, I wondered, *Why did I wait so long? I want to do that again!*

I am a slow learner, but I had learned another principle of Creative Followership:

Do not be easily discouraged.

Granny, I Hate My Job!

"Granny, I hate my job."

Marie Sommers listened on the phone as her granddaughter, Michelle, went on, "I hate this job. I don't like my boss, I don't like this company, and I don't like these people I am working with."

Michelle continued to express her frustration.

"This is nothing like what I expected, after four years of college preparation. I am sorry that I chose this profession for a career."

Two months ago, Michelle had graduated, and she was very pleased to have been hired by the company of her choice for her dream job.

Her grandmother responded, "Michelle, I am going to send you a book that I know will be helpful. Read it and try practicing what you find there, then call and let me know what you think about it."

Three weeks later, Michelle called.

"Granny, I am only halfway through the book, but I can tell you that this works! And Granny, my boss is not as bad as I had first thought, and I am beginning to like the people I work with. It's not such a bad place to work, after all, and I am beginning to like working here. Granny, thanks for sending me that book."

I really like to share Creative Followership with seniors. When I speak to them, they immediately understand the value of what I advocate. They have no doubts; their experience confirms that the principles of Creative Followership work. These are principles that they themselves used to guide themselves throughout their careers.

They recognize many of these as the good old commonsense principles that their grandparents taught them when they were youngsters. They express their enthusiasm for Creative Followership by buying my books by the handful and sending them to their grandchildren.

Grandparents know that these principles will work for anyone, at any level of responsibility, in any organization.

They worked for me!

They will work for you.

What If I Can't
Choose My Boss?

B rian was excited to update me on what had happened since I had last seen him. With a big smile, he said, "I got the job with the county police department!" Since he was a boy, he had wanted to be a policeman. Now his dream was becoming a reality.

Brian wanted to tell me all about his training, which was well under way. "I have never been so tired and sore from physical and mental exertion. I expected the physical to be tough, but I did not consider the mental." He said, "I am learning to really appreciate our Constitution! It is no surprise that a policeman needs to know the law, but I never anticipated the emphasis on knowing the Constitution. A policeman has to understand the rights of individuals as well as violations of the law."

Obviously, Brian was enthusiastic about his new role as a policeman.

Then he said, "In your book, you say that the first principle of Creative Followership is Choose Your Boss. As a policeman, I will not be able to choose my boss. Frankly, that worries me, because even though I like some of my potential bosses, there are some that I hope I don't have to work for."

I asked him, "Is there someone who would be your first choice?"

"Oh, yes! There is more than one that I would like to work with."

My next question was, "Have you told them that you would like to work for them?"

A big smile appeared on Brian's face. He said, "I could choose my boss by getting him to choose me!"

If you can't choose your boss, get your boss to choose you!

Choose your boss.

My First Memory of Truett Cathy

It was late on a Friday afternoon during 1960 when I called to tell Oleta, my wife, that I was on the way home.

"We have friends coming over this evening," she reminded me. "Stop and pick up something to eat. It has been a hectic day and I did not get to cook."

I stopped at the Dwarf Grill, even though it was slightly off my usual route home. We liked the food, and the owner and his employees were especially nice and friendly to their customers.

When I walked in the door, Truett Cathy, the owner, warmly greeted me. It seemed like Truett was always in his restaurant during the busy times, and Friday evening was one of his busiest times.

Truett chatted with me as he took my carryout order for Dwarfburgers. He asked, "How many people will be eating?" I answered, "There will six of us."

When he handed me the bag with my food, he also handed me a whole lemon meringue pie, and said, "Have your dessert on me."

I was flabbergasted! A whole lemon pie? Free?

Oleta and I did not eat there often, and Truett hardly

56

knew us. He bought restaurant supplies from the company where I worked, but he was not my customer.

It was not the first time we had greeted or spoken to each other, but it is my first definite memory of the person, Truett Cathy.

Why would he give me a whole lemon pie, free?

That Friday evening, two clear pictures of what made this man, Truett Cathy, a unique and successful business-man began to take shape.

Truett was kind. He truly enjoyed being thoughtful and generous.

In his sixty-nine years in the restaurant business, he gave away more food than most restaurateurs have sold.

He especially liked to give people his lemon meringue pies. They had a wonderful taste and were beautifully made. For his pies, he used freshly squeezed lemons and a piled-high, hand-sculpted, beautiful meringue topping that was so consistently and uniformly shaped that many people thought the pies must be made by a machine.

It was usual and frequent that Truett would visit the home of someone who was sick or just released from the hospital, or a family gathering after a funeral. When he went, he often took food, especially lemon meringue pies.

One time he carried food out and loaded it into his sta-tion wagon to take to someone sick at home. When he stopped for a traffic light, a man drove up beside him, honked his horn, and pointed to the roof of Truett's station wagon. When Truett pulled over to the curb and got out,

Chick-fil-A Lemon Meringue Pie

he found his lemon pie was still on the roof, but most of the meringue had been blown away!

Truett was a business builder.

His original Dwarf Grill restaurant location, opened in 1946, has been in operation for sixty-nine years. Sales have increased every year but one—the year his son, Bubba opened another Dwarf House nearby.

His first Chick-fil-A restaurant opened in 1967. Chick-fil-A sales have increased every year for forty-seven years.

I don't know if Truett was aware that I had never tasted his lemon meringue pie, the day he gave me the free pie. I have often wondered, but cannot remember: did he ask me if I had tried his lemon pie? Maybe he did. I am confident that I had never tasted them, because I thought I did not like lemon pie. I always chose chocolate or coconut pie when I went to his restaurant.

I do know that when Truett gave me that free pie, he left a permanent mark in my memory.

Truett Cathy was a kind and smart businessman.

I am glad that I chose a kind and smart businessman, Truett Cathy, for my boss.

Remember, Choose Your Boss is the first principle of Creative Followership.

Choose your boss.

Are You Blind
to Opportunities?

C an you see them? They are all around you. They are opportunities!

Are you aware of how many surround you each day? Many people miss out on great opportunities because they don't see them.

Creative Followership can open your eyes so that you can see the opportunities that are right in front of you. Uncover your eyes and take a look with me.

During my years in a senior executive role, fellow workers frequently came to me seeking promotions. When I asked why they wanted a promotion, I usually received one of two replies: "I want to make more money" or "I want more authority."

True or not, many people believe they are underpaid. How about you? Most people also believe they can handle the responsibility of more authority. How about you?

When someone said she wanted to make more money, I was certain that was exactly what she was thinking. I understood. Even though I have met a few people who said they were overpaid, I never believed they really meant it.

I don't remember anyone ever using the exact words,

"I want more authority." Most often, they used this approach: "Put me in charge and I will straighten out that department" or "If I was the boss I would . . ." Possibly, you have had similar thoughts.

My response was to ask, "What would you do?" Seldom did I get a well-thought-out answer with definite ideas. Usually, there was no plan of action, only an attitude of "I know I could do better than the boss." It is possible these people could have done better than the boss, but I had no way of knowing that.

I saw these sessions as Creative Followership coaching opportunities.

You don't have to be the boss or in another placement to perform at your best. There are opportunities all around you. Take action where you are. You probably already have plenty of authority and all the freedom you need to get started.

Don't be concerned that the boss will get credit for your initiative or creativity. The more you assume responsibility and help your boss to be successful, the more likely you are to get outstanding performance reviews and a higher income. The largest income increases and the best promotions go to the boss's dedicated followers.

If you work for a smart boss, your boss will know you are helping him or her to succeed, and your help will be welcomed. Supporting your boss, promoting her agenda, and taking more responsibility will raise the value of your service. As your boss advances in the organization, you want to be recognized as one of the most effective and loyal followers so that the boss will take you along.

Of course, if you work for a boss who is not very smart, this will not work. If you work for a boss lacking in intelligence or integrity, you should fire that boss, after you find a smart one you can respect.

Creative followers don't need to ask for more authority. They earn more authority by taking on additional responsibility. They receive more and bigger income increases because they earn them.

Help your boss succeed.

Do you see now?

Look! Do you see all of those opportunities to help your boss succeed?

When you help the boss succeed, you will board his or her train and you will enjoy the ride together.

Help your boss succeed.

Dealing with Personal Discouragement

Dealing with personal discouragement is tough for most people. Discouragement can drag you down quickly, unless you learn to deal with it in a positive manner.

At a young age, I realized that everyone I know faces some form of discouragement in life. I also noticed that a person could control how discouragement affected his or her life. By the time I reached high school, I had decided that in the face of discouragement I would remind myself, "I am not easily discouraged." It was amazing how that helped me through difficult times.

Overcoming discouragement is often a topic of interest when I speak to young people, and I like to tell them the following story.

When I was a teenager, during the fabulous fifties, my friends and I visited drive-in restaurants several evenings during the week. This really was a popular thing to do; it was much like a scene from the movies *American Graffiti* and *Grease*.

A friend of mine was dating a girl from Brown High School, a school not far from ours. We frequently spotted a gray Buick full of girls from Brown at a drive-in called

Oleta McKibben and Jimmy Collins
June 6, 1954

Uncle Tom's. My friend's girlfriend and her sister, Oleta McKibben, were usually in that car. Oleta was the prettiest of those Brown High girls! She was spunky and I liked her.

Immediately, however, I faced discouragement. Oleta did not like me! Even though I tried my best to turn on the charm and my most likable personality, nothing seemed to work with her. She was not impressed.

I wanted Oleta to go out with me, but I suspected she might turn me down. I did not want to face outright rejection, so I asked a friend of hers to check and see whether Oleta would say yes if I asked her out. Her friend came back with "She is not interested."

I really liked Oleta and did not want to give up, so I asked my friend who was dating Oleta's sister to see if he could arrange a double date with Oleta and me. Again, word came back, "She is not interested."

Then I learned that she was having a birthday party. I was certain I could find a way to get invited. I asked her sister to get me an invitation. Just like before, the word was "She is not interested."

Well, I reminded myself, I am not easily discouraged. So I went anyway!

The next weekend, on June 6, 1954, we had our first date. After that day, I never dated another girl. For more sixty years, Oleta has been the most important person in my life, my most trusted adviser, my greatest encourager, and my wife.

I have often thought how different my life would have been if I had become discouraged, had given up, and had not gone uninvited to that birthday party. I think of how much I would have missed, how much less fulfilling my life would have been!

It would be impossible to count how many times I have reminded myself, "I am not easily discouraged." Hundreds—maybe thousands. This reminder has become a Creative Followership principle.

Do not be easily discouraged.

It is a principle that has affected my life positively more times than I can count. There have been occasions when I used it several times during a single week.

It is my choice; I will not be easily discouraged.

It could be your choice!

Do not be easily discouraged.

Be Thankful for Strong-Willed Critics

Most people do not like strong-willed critics who question their actions, hold them accountable, or express opposing views.

That is unfortunate, because they are missing out on an opportunity for growth.

That's right! Strong-willed criticism is a wonderful opportunity for self-development, and those who avoid it will never know what they missed.

All of my life, I have enjoyed a good fight. (That is, as long as there is no physical pain for anyone, nor any blood shed—especially mine!)

What I enjoy about a fight of ideas, when aggressively slugged out with a passionate and well-rehearsed opponent in one corner and me in the opposite, is that it clarifies my thinking. A worthy opponent can cause me to understand his position, provide an opportunity for me to clarify my own position, and offer a chance to weigh the benefits of different ideas.

Only after I test my position in this way am I prepared to preach, practice, and persuade others to accept my position. It is a healthy process that must be faced head-on and never avoided.

Let me give you an example.

During my late twenties and early thirties, I taught a Sunday school class for young married couples at my church. We were all about the same age and most of us had young children. There were sharp people in that class, and many of them were comfortable enough to speak up or disagree.

I was blessed to have one special person in the class—let's call him Joe. He was an airline pilot, and when he entered his cockpit he was fully prepared to fly. He expected no less of his teacher.

Joe was intelligent, had an almost photographic memory, could debate skillfully, and knew a great deal about the Bible. Along with several others, he made certain that I tied up all the loose ends in my lesson presentations.

Joe was the one most responsible for holding me accountable, pushing me to grow and develop into a more effective teacher. He motivated me to always be at my best, and I had to invest more time in the preparation for this class because the focus was not only on what to say to the class—the lesson also had to be prepared in a way that was acceptable to Joe. The process inspired me personally and spiritually.

Thank God for the many friends like Joe I have had in my life over the years.

Be thankful for strong-willed critics.

At Chick-fil-A, we attracted many independent-minded,

entrepreneurial, and high-spirited Operators. I loved them! They were mustangs—people who lived on the edge of, and sometimes beyond, their authority. Mustangs charge and pull ahead very quickly, and some Operators pulled really hard.

That was okay with me! I appreciated this kind the most. The scuffles were productive, and we all grew and profited from them. They stimulated my personal and professional growth.

I am thankful for the mustangs in my life.

Be thankful for strong-willed critics.

Some people prefer dealing with milder, more submissive personalities who do not tend to make waves. However, few things change if everyone is concerned about maintaining the status quo. Mustangs get ahead faster because mustangs take charge and move things forward.

As a creative follower, be an example—be a mustang! Think for yourself, push the envelope, and live on the edge of your authority. You are much more valuable on the leading edge than you are in a safer, more sedate place where nothing much happens.

At the same time, take it a step further; cultivate and encourage mustangs to keep you on your toes. And . . .

Be thankful for strong-willed critics.

The Only Real Feedback

I was in a hurry to leave the church. The worship service was over; it had met my expectations. The music, a blend of contemporary and traditional, was okay. The preacher's illustrations and sermon had clearly communicated a good message. Everything had occurred in an orderly and timely manner.

I just had time to make it to my lunch appointment.

As I was on my way through the parking lot, heading toward my car, someone called from behind me, "Jimmy, wait a minute." It was Ray Davis, the man who manages the sound system.

"How was the sound in your section this morning?" he asked. I had not even noticed. He continued, "Finally, I figured out why we were having so much trouble in the section where you sit, and I fixed it." I had not even noticed that the sound was perfect that morning.

We don't usually notice when things happen perfectly, do we? Perfect is what we expect.

At our church, we have an old sound system that has been pieced together and patched over the years, to the point where it is difficult to keep it operating effectively.

Because we plan to relocate in the near future, it would not be good stewardship to buy a new system, so Ray and his helpers do the best they can with what we have. In the section where my family sits, the sound often was very poor and detracted from the service. When it was not working right, I told Ray.

When I was back at the church later that week, I went to Ray and thanked him for resolving that problem. I apologized for always complaining when things were not right, then not recognizing the perfect sound we now had in my section.

Ray said, "I need you to tell me when the sound is not right. Otherwise, I won't know about it and can't fix it. I need your negative feedback."

Think about what Ray said. He needs negative feedback.

Positive feedback does not motivate us to do anything different or better. Positive feedback just makes us complacent and satisfied that everything is okay.

We all need negative feedback. It is the only feedback we can really use to improve our performance. Negative feedback is the only real feedback.

Ray Davis knows what he is talking about. We all need to listen.

The only real feedback is negative.

The practice of this principle will enhance your career and build your reputation.

The Most Important Decisions

Wearing glasses with lenses as thick as the bottom of old-fashioned Coca-Cola bottles, the old professor sat on the edge of an ancient wooden desk, his hands gripping the edge of the top while he swung his feet back and forth. Sitting was appropriate for a man of 86 years with a replacement hip only seven weeks old. That was why he was sitting, rather than walking around, as he accepted questions from the audience in the crowded conference room.

A young man asked, "Mr. Drucker, what is the most important decision an executive must make?"

Peter Drucker replied, "The most important decisions that executives make are people decisions."

His advice resonates in my mind today, as if he had just said it a minute ago. I not only still hear him saying it, but also the memories of the hundreds of confirmations that I have experienced serve as echoes returning from the walls of the canyon of time.

I think not only of the confirmation that results from the good decisions. Those are like the pleasant, soft murmurs stirred by a summer breeze, compared with the damage resulting from the bad decisions. Like destructive storms, bad people decisions sometimes do irreparable damage, often leaving a trail of disappointment and grief.

During my career at Chick-fil-A, I was keenly interested in who was selected to become a franchisee or staff employee. In the early days, when I helped Operators open their restaurants, I was also actively involved in coaching them in their employee selections.

I was often asked, "Jimmy, why do you spend so much of your time on the selection process?" My answer was, "I don't have anything more important to do."

I was approaching retirement before I heard Peter Drucker's wise advice. But I had listened to other wise teachers of business practice, and I had seen the reality of good and bad people decisions.

If we listen to the lessons of experience—our own as well as that of others—we will learn what is most important. However, unless you put it into practice, learning is worthless, and a waste of time. Creative followers spend whatever time and energy is necessary to make certain that every people decision is a good one.

Whether you are the final decision maker or a contributor to the process of people decisions, your role is very important. You may know, learn, or suspect something of critical importance to the selection of a new employee or potential transferee.

Many times, the receptionist or the driver who picked up an interview candidate at the airport gave me valuable input on that candidate. I solicited and encouraged everyone who came in contact with franchisee and job candidates to make their impressions known to the decision makers. Even though they had no involvement in the final decision, their contributions were very important.

Whatever your level of responsibility, remember:

The most important decisions are people decisions.

That Is Unnecessary

How many of these have you seen? I have seen signs like this in many places. Most often, they mark sidewalks that will never be used, simply because they go nowhere that people are likely to walk.

Signs like this one are easy to see. They are posted where every passing citizen can be made aware of the lack of commonsense efficiency that prevails in the administration of many government agencies. They make us wonder why someone doesn't do something about it.

Have you thought about how many unnecessary signs you encounter that are not so obvious? If you work for an organization that has two or more people and has been in operation for one year, you have unnecessary work being done. Does that seem like an exaggeration? The smile on your face confirms that you know it is not.

How much unnecessary work is going on in your organization? What is being done today because at some time in the past it seemed like a good idea? What reports are being prepared that no one reads? What work contributes nothing or very little to the purpose and mission of your organization? These all are signs of unnecessary work.

Sign on Georgia Highway 74

Creative followers see these unnecessary signs. They see the signs and take action to eliminate that unnecessary work.

What can you do? You can do plenty! Find out why something is being done, when it started, and if it is achieving the desired results. If not, see that this activity is eliminated.

Take Responsibility.

If you don't have the authority to do it alone, enlist supporters and then present your case to the person who does have the authority and who is most likely to take action. Before you present your case for action, build support among those most likely to have a stake in eliminating (or retaining) what you want to eliminate.

Here are some important clues. Contact the person most likely to be able to influence the one in authority.

And don't forget the person most likely to oppose you. Find out if he or she will support or resist your efforts. Ask for advice on how best to accomplish what you want to do. That is how you build support, and you want to know where you stand before you make your case for action.

Build Support in Advance.

Every good boss knows that her workers have a production limit and that the easiest way to get more productivity is to eliminate the unnecessary or less important work.

Good bosses are leaders looking for creative followers to help them be successful. Work to make your boss more successful by eliminating the unnecessary. Your boss will value you and will want you on his or her train to success.

Eliminate the unnecessary.

Help your boss succeed.

Everybody Likes Problems

My boss said, "I don't like problems."
I didn't believe him!
I like problems. You like problems. Everybody likes problems!

Think about it. We all like problems.

My boss just wanted to pick and choose his problems. Truett Cathy was a great problem solver, but he was particular about how he spent his time and about which problems he concentrated on solving.

At this point, are you a believer or a doubter?

Have you ever gone fishing? Which was more fun—catching the little fish that gulped down your hook and jumped into the boat, or that big fighter that almost wore you out before you got it into the boat? Think of your most satisfying accomplishments. Were they easy tasks or the most difficult problems you've ever encountered? Every time you look back and relive the experience in your memory, don't you think about what a great time that was? Are you with me now?

When I finally understood that my boss liked to *choose* his problems, I created this game plan: if I solve those problems that my boss does not like to deal with, I can add a lot of value to Chick-fil-A, and there might not be a limit to what my boss will pay me.

Really good problem solvers can name their own price. Surely you don't doubt that. Which athletes are able to negotiate the highest compensation? Wouldn't you call them problem solvers?

Be a problem solver! Believe me. This will work. It is Creative Followership.

It works best when you choose a boss who does not like to do the things you do very well. Choose the right boss and then go to work on solving problems.

It is the most direct route to success and satisfaction in any organization.

Do what your boss does not like to do.

Let Others See the Boss in You

I worked for Truett Cathy for thirty-two years. Many people have asked, "How did you create such a good working relationship with Truett?"

I tell them I practiced Creative Followership.

What I practiced, you can practice. It will work for anyone, at any level of responsibility, in any organization. It will work for you.

My goal was to support my boss in such a way that whatever I did was what the boss would have done, yet I never tried to give my actions more weight by using the boss's name. When things did not go right, I never blamed the boss. I took responsibility myself and went to work to do whatever was necessary to correct the situation.

Others never knew whether a decision was Truett's or mine. When I disagreed with Truett on something, I never disclosed these private interactions. Furthermore, I never told anyone when Truett overruled me. I never said, "We are doing this because this is what the boss wants."

Those times when I was overruled were no one else's business; they were between Truett and me. There was much more to gain by keeping them close to the vest—

and there was potentially everything to lose by recklessly discussing them with someone else.

My objective was to let others see the boss in me.

I let others see the boss in me not because I could not make decisions or act independently but to present a unified purpose and action. When people in an organization see management in unity, they have more confidence in their own roles. They know that management is in harmony and feel empowered to follow that example.

Your work should mirror the quality and character of the boss. I do not think I need to explain every detail of how to do this. It is another instance where every situation is unique. If you have what it takes to be a creative follower, you can certainly work it out.

If you have picked a leader you can follow, surely you have picked a boss of excellence. Do things in a manner that will meet and even exceed your leader's personal standards. When you can do this proficiently, you have assumed an indispensable role for the leader. You have moved beyond just being a worker; you are now a follower of your leader.

I urge you not to buy into the misconception of a follower as someone who is led mindlessly around by another person. Far from being a demeaning, subservient role, followership places the creative follower in a position to greatly profit from the relationship, professionally, personally, and financially.

As King Solomon puts it (Proverbs 27:18):

He who tends the fig tree will eat its fruit,
And he who cares for his master will be honored

The follower who has made the boss look good and has done the things the boss does not like to do—or does not do well—eventually finds him- or herself in a position to influence where the whole organization is going.

Is that the role you seek? If so,

Let others see the boss in you.

Always Apologize;
Never Explain

Customer complaints are an excellent source of feedback. Therefore, a customer complaint represents a colossal opportunity.

It is a shame that the opportunity usually turns into a dismal disappointment for both parties, because it does not have to be that way. Customer complaints can end with the customer walking away with a more favorable impression of the organization, and the organization can learn lessons that may prevent the same thing from happening in the future.

There is a right way and a wrong way to deal with complaints.

First, when dealing with customer complaints, I *always apologize*.

I find that the following procedure works best: I apologize, whether the problem is my fault or not—I have a no-fault apology policy. I deliver the apology as if I am the only one responsible. I take responsibility, and even if the customer is wrong, mistaken, or unreasonable, I treat the customer as if he or she is right and reasonable.

Second, I make it a point to *never explain* anything.

I do not give details about why something happened this way or that way. This is a good policy whether you are dealing with customers or are approaching the boss about some business matter. I do not give reasons because the customer doesn't want to hear it.

As soon as you start to explain, the customer perceives that you are attempting to defend yourself, your fellow workers, your boss, or your company. It appears to the complainant that you are avoiding responsibility for what has happened and that you are making the customer out to be the offender, the one who has disturbed the peace.

Rather than offering a defense, I ask the customer to explain how the situation looked and felt to him or her, and then I ask for suggestions on how to avoid repeating this situation in the future.

Next, I turn the table and *put the customer in charge* by asking what he or she would consider a suitable response for this unfortunate situation.

I ask, "What would you like me to do?" After the customer makes a suggestion, I try to exceed expectations and do more than was asked.

Again, this is just good practice. When dealing with critical feedback, apologize, fix the problem, and exceed expectations.

Leave a positive impression and you can learn from the criticism, because all negative feedback is beneficial.

Perhaps you do not work in a retail situation, with the public, or with customers. You do, however, have a boss.

And if you work for a boss, the boss is your customer! This principle works equally well with those in authority.

I have found that, like customers, the boss usually does not want an explanation. Even if the boss asks for an explanation, that is not what he or she wants. An explanation sounds defensive and evasive, neither of which the boss wants to hear.

Take responsibility, apologize, and fix the situation the way the boss likes it done.

Always apologize; never explain.

Rules Are Like Rabbits

"**R**abbits do not make good pets!" my father said emphatically.

"Daddy, please! They are so cute and cuddly—they won't be any trouble," I pleaded.

"They are nothing but trouble. You will see and be sorry," he said as he relented.

Oh, how I wish we had listened! I wish I had paid attention to his advice before we got the rabbits.

Today, I am reminded that rules and regulations are like rabbits. Like rabbits, rules do not make good pets.

First, rabbits may look cute and have soft fur, but they are a lot of trouble. Rules look like a good idea until you get them. Like rabbits, rules appear attractive, but they are difficult to manage, interpret, and enforce in the real world. ***Rules are like rabbits.***

Second, my father warned my siblings and me, but we did not listen. He said, "You can train a dog, and even a cat to some degree, but it is impossible to train a rabbit to do anything." He was right. Rabbits are virtually untrainable, and they leave a mess wherever they go.

Rules are like that, too. In the beginning, they seem

like useful controls, but they always come with unexpected consequences. You think rules will work to your advantage and help the organization, but they end up creating new problems and fail to solve the old ones.

Rules are like rabbits.

Third, growing up in the country, my father hunted wild rabbits for food. He said, "Rabbits are good to eat, but that's about all they are good for." I don't know if they are good to eat or not; I could never bring myself to accept the idea of eating rabbit meat. I could not stomach the idea. The same can be said about rules. You may have positive expectation for rules, but when you get a taste of all the problems they generate, you may find them too hard to swallow.

Rules are like rabbits.

Finally, the most obvious thing about rabbits is how fast they multiply. Those two rabbits that we had in the beginning quickly reproduced, and then we had a dozen. We not only ended up with more rabbits than we wanted but also, when we tried to get rid of a few, we found that no one wanted any rabbits. We could not get rid of them.

Rules are like rabbits: you may begin with only one or two, thinking that will be all you are going to need, but that is not the way it works. Right away you will need several new rules to clarify the first few, then a couple more to smooth out those bumps in the process. They tend to multiply quickly. Nobody wants more rules and regulations. Not only do the rules and regulations multiply; their caregivers also multiply. The more rules an organization

has, the more people are required to enforce them. Like rabbits, it is nearly impossible to get rid of rules once you give them a home.

Rules are like rabbits.

We don't need more rules; we need clear and simple principles to guide us.

Rules complicate. Principles clarify.

Before you even think of advocating another rule, remember . . .

Rules are like rabbits!

Enhance your career, advocate principles, and eliminate rules.

Adapters and Adopters

When I received the e-mail, I chuckled. Even though I had been asked the question before, I had never been given a choice of two answers.

The question was: "What two innovations do you claim credit for during your thirty-two years at Chick-fil-A?"

My answer was in the same spirit that I always respond: "None."

Even though many people may claim credit for many inventions, innovations, and originations, I don't claim any. My experience confirms the truth of the proverb that there is nothing new under the sun.

Rarely can anyone truly claim the discovery, invention, or origination of anything. Think about it. Can you claim the invention of anything? Do you know anyone who can?

Does it really matter? Yes!

If you are focused on gaining recognition, you will lose. You will lose the cooperation of your coworkers. You will lose the support of those reporting to you. You will lose the endorsement of your boss.

No one enjoys working with a glory seeker.

Here is the way I dealt with this issue. It worked for

me, and I believe it will work for you.

Even though I am not an inventor, innovator, or originator, I am an adapter and adopter. Often, I see, hear, or learn something that stimulates my thinking along this line. I see packaging for a product unrelated to food service that gives me an idea of how a similar process could be adapted for quick-service food. I hear about the results of a demographic study that defines how a certain market segment makes purchasing decisions, and this stimulates my thinking about an improved marketing approach for potential customers in that market segment. I learn of a military training program that franchisees could adopt to train their restaurant supervisors.

Am I functioning as an inventor, innovator, or originator? No. I am an adapter and adopter.

All of us adapt and adopt. We all do it, but some do it better than others. That is why I shared my observations, ideas, and suggestions with people who might be able to help me.

When one person lights a spark, another adds tinder to start a flame, another lays on a little kindling, and another adds a dry log, together they can build a great bonfire.

Who built the fire? Who was the innovator? Is it the one providing the spark, or is it the one providing the tinder, the kindling, or the dry log?

To be a successful adapter and adopter, you need this mind-set.

Share your ideas with others who can help you achieve your objective, but share it in such a way that it will become *their* objective. In addition, you want them to know, without question, that you will take the blame for the consequences of failure.

Share the credit; accept the blame.

When you are willing to share the credit for success and accept the blame for failure, people will gladly join you in adapting and adopting.

Negative Feedback

A new supervisor and I discussed his staff's response to his new management role.

"They are very satisfied," he said. "Everything is going great."

I asked, "How do you know?"

He answered, "I know because there has been no negative feedback, only positive."

"You are in real trouble," I told him. "You must create an environment that permits, invites, and values negative feedback."

No matter how good you are as a supervisor, there is never a time when everything is good and positive. There are always problems, dysfunctional processes, and burdensome rules. Even if you have only one person reporting to you, that person actually doing the work knows ways to improve productivity and morale that you have not and probably never will think about.

Positive feedback may make a supervisor feel good, but it is worthless. It just encourages you to continue what you are doing, to maintain the status quo. There is nothing to encourage or motivate improvement.

If you really do want to improve the productivity and morale of your staff, create an environment in which everyone knows you are open to negative feedback and suggestions for improvement.

They will only know this if you tell them, in no uncertain terms. You must understand that you will have to say this over and over and over again. They will only believe it when they see you actually practice what you preach. Only when you recognize those who speak out and tell you the truth, only when they see that nothing negative happens to those who tell you what you don't want to hear, and only when they see you set a new direction based on their negative feedback will they believe you.

The only real feedback is negative.

Only negative feedback provides opportunities and direction for improvement. From it, you have usable material to set new paths and invent new and better processes.

Play it smart. Seek negative feedback!

Be Thankful for
a Do-Nothing Boss

As we have seen, one of the most important principles of Creative Followership is:
Do what your boss does not like to do.

There are other, related principles. Even though they are practical and effective when understood, I have found that many employees are surprised when I explain them. But because the purpose and execution are so clear, simple, and practical, the principles are enthusiastically received when explained.

Before I retired, when I was providing supervision training for Chick-fil-A franchisee restaurant employees, I liked to ask, "Do you work for a boss who does not like to do much?"

Usually, after a hesitant glance around the room, someone would say, "Yes, I do." Once the first person said yes, everyone in the class would boldly agree.

My next question always surprised the listeners. I would ask, "Do you realize how fortunate you are? Just think of the opportunity this leaves open for you."

In most classes, someone would say, "How about me? My boss does not like to do *anything*!" And I would tell him or her, honestly, "Your opportunities are unlimited." I was not being ironic; it is a true statement. An inexperienced employee may not realize that a leader will leave a follower a lot of opportunities to express him- or herself. A worker will shirk the responsibility and wait for instructions. A creative follower, on the other hand, will grab the opportunity and run with it.

When, as a creative follower, you do what the boss does not like to do—and do it well—you add value. The more you do what the boss does not like to do, the more valuable you become. Your opportunities to get the prime assignments, excellent performance reviews, and larger pay increases are greatly enhanced.

That is why you should be thankful for a do-nothing boss. The less the boss likes to do, the greater your opportunities.

It amazes me when employees spend time complaining that "my boss does not do any work." It is puzzling, because what people usually mean is that the boss is not joining them in doing the kind of work the employees are paid to do. But the boss must not duplicate the tasks assigned to other workers.

There are times when a good boss will step in to help employees at critical moments, but employees should realize that if a boss is duplicating the tasks the workers are doing, then the boss is neglecting the job the boss is being paid to do.

In this situation, a creative follower will help the boss

get back to his or her management position and the responsibilities of that job.

Be thankful for a do-nothing boss.

You have a great opportunity. Take advantage of it!

Do what your boss does not like to do.

Bottom-Up Thinking

The radio host introduced me as the author of *Creative Followership: In the Shadow of Greatness*, and his first interview question for me was, "How is Creative Followership different from leadership?"

That is a question I often hear.

For some reason, many people just cannot think about career relationships without determining what form of leadership is involved.

My answer is, "Creative Followership is *bottom-up* thinking."

The blank stares from mystified eyes are my signal to continue, and I do. "Leadership-oriented thinking is *top-down* thinking."

Think about that for a moment. Picture the organization as a pyramid, with the leader at the apex and the followers forming the rest of the pyramid.

Creative followers are practicing bottom-up thinking. Their focus is on supporting and boosting the leader up higher to raise the performance level of the organization.

Typical leadership training, on the other hand, emphasizes top-down thinking. The concept is to look down, reach down, and drag up individual followers below to raise the performance level of the organization.

Now, be honest with yourself. Which is more likely to result in a more unified and higher-performing organization? Will it be the one where *many followers* are practicing bottom-up thinking, or the one where the *leader* is using top-down thinking?

I place my bets on the organization with many creative followers practicing bottom-up thinking!

This illustration won't answer every question, but it should give you a clear insight into the value of Creative Followership.

Bottom-up thinking.

I practiced it!

It worked for me!

It will work for anyone, at any level of responsibility, in any organization.

It will work for you!

There Are No Perfect Decisions

People ask me, "How do you make good decisions?" I have learned that the issue is not about making good decisions. The issue is how to make your decisions good.

There is no such thing as a perfect decision. You know this even though you may not have given it much thought. Think about it now.

If, following a decision, everything in the world were to stand still and not change for however many days it took for that decision to be fully complete and all the results to be known, you could possibly say, "I have made a good decision." However, we live in a dynamic world of change and motion, a place where nothing ever stays perfectly still. Think about how many unknown factors and people are likely to weigh in on your decision (including people who help you carry out your decision).

By the time you begin the execution of your well-thought-out plan, the original conditions have probably already changed significantly. Decision making is most often a process of making corrections and adjustments to the original plan to make it successful. Implementation requires many modifications.

It is not so much a matter of following a certain process to be sure you are making a good decision. Instead, it is a matter of making your decisions good.

Can you remember a single decision that worked out exactly as you first expected? I can't!

I have read books and sat through seminars about decision making. I vividly recall one presentation about how to make good decisions. All sorts of diagrams were presented, featuring everything from complex matrix systems to simple two-column pro-and-con lists. These supposedly provided details about how to weigh this side and that side of a decision-making equation, but there was no way I was going to be able to use that type of system. For me, all of the many different processes and systems designed to help a person make good decisions have something in common: I could never make a decision using any of them! These processes do not work for me, and they probably won't work for you.

Even the best-laid plans have to be modified. Some decisions are point-blank and have immediate consequences. But most decisions are measured by delayed or long-term results. It is the small but creative adjustments made along the way that make the difference between success and failure.

General Dwight D. Eisenhower said, *In preparing for battle I have always found that plans are useless but planning is indispensable.* He must have been thinking of all the adjustments to his plan that were necessary to make good his decision to invade Normandy on D-day, June 6, 1944.

Here is what I have concluded about decision making: you have to take responsibility for making a decision good by constantly nurturing it, guiding it, and reevaluating the intermediate results to see whether it is taking you where you wanted to go. Circumstances are always changing; unforeseen obstacles, opportunities, and adversities happen.

Don't give up, don't give in, and be flexible in the execution, to fit the situation. It is up to you, and it is an active process.

Make your decisions good.

Nothing Happens Until Somebody Sells Something

I am amazed that some people have such a difficult time determining what is important to the organization that provides their employment.

Most of us view the organization we work for by what radiates from our position. For the receptionist, a warm, friendly, helpful greeting to all visitors is most important. For an accountant, accurate bookkeeping is the center of and most important activity. For the person in the warehouse, it is accurate and careful receiving, storing, and shipping of merchandise. For the lawyer, nothing is more important than well-worded and properly executed documents.

What is most important to your organization, to any organization, to every organization?

The answer is simple and clear:

Nothing happens until somebody sells something.

Think about it.

Before I retired from Chick-fil-A, I emphasized, more than anything else, this simple statement: "If you are not selling chicken, you'd better be supporting someone who is!"

Until somebody sold chicken, I was not needed. Until somebody sold chicken, there was no need for any home office employees. Until somebody sold chicken, there was no need for managers or any other workers in the restaurants.

At the time I retired, there were 30,000 people employed by Chick-fil-A, its franchisees, and its affiliates. The number is more than 70,000 today. And not a single one of us was needed until somebody sold chicken.

That's why I continuously reminded myself and every person within the organization, "If you are not selling chicken, you'd better be supporting someone who is."

Your organization only needs you to sell or support whatever you provide. It may be a product or a service. Before you ask, the answer is the same even if you work for a nonprofit or government organization.

Think about it.

Are you selling health care, mail delivery, bus rides, entertainment, shoes, insurance, groceries, or government services? If you are not the one selling the product or service, you'd better be supporting somebody who is.

Nothing happens until somebody sells something.

No employee is needed until somebody sells something. If you are not selling, your purpose is to support the person who is selling.

Once a product or service is sold, everyone should be focused on producing and delivering the product or service and serving the customer.

This is simple. Don't complicate it with endless buts and what-ifs.

Remember: if you are not selling [your product or service], you'd better be supporting someone who is!

Do Not Compete
with Your Boss

I vividly recall one afternoon when I returned to the Chick-fil-A home office after speaking at a local Kiwanis luncheon. When I saw Truett, I told him what a fine reception I had received, thinking he would be pleased by the positive emotional connection I had created for Chick-fil-A among those present at the luncheon.

Though he was usually predictable, his reaction that day was not what I had anticipated. He said, "You could get a speaking engagement every day. They are easy to get, because all organizations have someone responsible for finding speakers."

Truett was correct. People were constantly calling to ask him to speak. At that time, he was averaging two speaking engagements per week.

He went on, "You leave the speaking to me and concentrate on the business."

Truett liked to speak, and he was an excellent communicator. By putting myself out there as an available public speaker, I had violated my own Creative Followership Principle 3: Do What Your Boss Does Not Like to Do, and Principle 4: Do What Your Boss Does Not Do Well. That day I added my fifth principle of Creative Followership: *Do not compete with your boss.*

From that day forward, I did not accept a business-oriented speaking engagement. I knew that Chick-fil-A only needed one spokesperson speaker. I focused on the business and left the speaking to Truett.

I chose to step back out of the spotlight and into Truett's shadow.

In that shadow, I focused on what Truett did not like to do and what he did not do well. I freed him to do what he liked to do and what he did well. That made him more productive. I was adding value to the business, and it also made me more valuable. I was a supporter, not a competitor.

As a follower, you will be called upon to make this decision from time to time. You will need to determine what is in your best interest. Are you prepared to venture out on your own? Are you prepared to find a new boss? Is it better to work in the shadow of your leader?

I was convinced that my future was brighter in Truett's shadow.

As a follower, you must never put yourself in competition with your leader. Remember your role as the follower: to work for the boss, not against the boss or in competition with the boss.

No matter how tempting it may be to draw attention to yourself, the competition is fixed; you will not come out the winner. Just continue to remind yourself of the larger

Clipping from The Newnan Times-Herald

picture and why you do what you do—you have chosen a boss to stand behind and support. The more you promote the boss, the more success you create for the boss, the more you succeed as well.

Get on the right boss's train and it will take you where you want to go.

Do not compete with your boss.

Everybody Knows

When wise men speak, are you listening? When your coworkers know, do you know?

Here is what I have heard wise men say.

Peter Drucker:

The most important decisions executives make are people decisions.

Charles "Red" Scott:

Hire smart rather than manage tough.

S. Truett Cathy:

Select the right person and you will eliminate most of your problems.

I listened. Are you listening?

Making people decisions starts with *who*. They continue with *who* does *what*.

No matter what level of responsibility you have, you will be called upon to make people decisions. Before you face the reality of "do it now," prepare for what will be the most important decisions of your career.

Start with *who*. You absolutely must pick the best person available. Yes, the best *available*. You cannot expect to have the best in the world as a choice. Even so, your choice, whether good or bad, will make (or break) your reputation for effectiveness as an executive.

Next, who does *what*? People decisions begin with *who*, but they mean nothing until implemented, when you decide *what* that person will do. If you select the right person to do the right job, your reputation will be enhanced. If you pick the wrong person, you will suffer the consequences.

You may be selecting a person to do a specific task, to supervise a group, to train a new employee, to handle a customer complaint, or to take on a job with more responsibility. It does not matter what the people decision is, choose wisely.

Such choices often require "the wisdom of Solomon." You won't often have choices between great and awful. Instead, your choices will have to be made after careful evaluation of small differentials in knowledge or skill. But if that is the sum total of what you must measure, you will usually be pleased with the result. The real test is how you deal with personality, character, experience, and that critical factor, creativity. What will happen if the situation does not work out according to the initial plan? How will the person you selected deal with the unexpected?

Does this seem like a lot to consider? Yes, it is, and you must keep in mind the most important factor of all: who will evaluate your performance? If you make a good people decision, who will know? Your coworkers will know. Your customers will know. Your boss will know.

Everybody will know!

If you make a bad people decision, who will know? Everybody will know!

The most important decisions are people decisions.

Enhance your career by preparing for and making good people decisions. The most respected and valuable people in any organization are those who make good people decisions.

The Best Career Advice, Ever!

I want to share with you the best career advice I ever received.

As a youngster, I was constantly searching for career advice, tips, and directions on the best ways to advance my career. I read books, listened to cassette tapes, and attended seminars, searching for the secrets to success.

After a while, it finally dawned on me that there are no secrets. During my search, I did learn a lot that I found useful, but something was missing. I needed a personal mission statement that would guide me.

When I finally found this advice, from the wisest man who ever lived, King Solomon, I knew immediately that it was perfect to guide my career. I wholeheartedly recommend it to you.

He who tends the fig tree will eat its fruit,
And he who cares for his master will be honored.

This is Proverbs 27:18. Think though it with me.

He who tends the fig tree . . .

That is very clear. If you want the figs, you have to tend the tree—fertilize it, water it, prune it.

Will eat its fruit, . . .

The person who tends that tree will eat its fruit—that

is, enjoy the results of his labor.

And he who cares for his master . . .

Obviously, the master, in today's terminology, is the boss. Thus, it is also essential that you care for the boss. You are taking responsibility for the boss's interest, the fig tree.

Will be honored.

The person who cares for the boss's interests will be *honored.* When you take care of the boss's interests, you will get the good performance reviews, prime assignments, best raises, and promotions.

Surely you will see, as I did, the easy application of this simple and clear advice to your own career.

I never worked for a boss who had fig trees, but they all had a business that I was hired to tend. My first boss, Mr. Brown, had a neighborhood grocery store, and my last boss, Truett Cathy, had Chick-fil-A restaurants.

By tending Mr. Brown's store and Truett Cathy's restaurants, I was able to enjoy the fruit of my labor; they paid me from their profits.

As a result of taking care of Truett Cathy and his interests, my absolute loyalty was rewarded by his unwavering support, and I was honored appropriately.

King Solomon's wise advice defines Creative Followership. It will work for anyone, at any level of responsibility, in any organization. It worked for me! It will work for you!

He who tends the fig tree will eat its fruit,
And he who cares for his master will be honored.
The best career advice, ever!

Nobody Notices Perfect

Nobody notices perfect. Everybody notices imperfect. Surely, you know this. I do . . . and I don't like it. Yet I am as guilty of it as everyone else.

When everything works like it is supposed to, my expectations have been met, and I am satisfied. Why should I consider that unusual or worthy of my attention? Isn't that the way the world and all of its parts are supposed to work? Of course it is!

That is the way I look at the world when others are creating the perfect experiences for me to enjoy. Don't you?

What grabs my attention is when something is not perfect.

By nature, I am a critic. It is just part of my DNA. No matter where I go or what I do, the flaws, the mistakes, the disorder, the crooked picture, the sloppy paint job, the dirty fork, the missing letter, or the misspelled word catch my attention.

Unless I have completely misunderstood my observations over seventy-nine years, most of you are fellow critics by nature. Do you see the perfect or the imperfect?

I seldom recognize the perfect performance.

If you do something perfectly, don't expect to receive praise or congratulations. All you did is what was expected of you. Praise is not the usual reward for perfect performance. The reward for perfect performance is *personal satisfaction!* You know when you do it right. Personal satisfaction keeps us doing whatever we do, perfectly. Yes, an advanced degree of maturity and self-confidence make this easier. Do it perfectly and relish the satisfaction of doing it right.

When you perform perfectly, don't expect to be recognized or even noticed. Whether you cut hair, cook hamburgers, replace worn-out knees, land an airplane, deliver the mail, or change a diaper, do it right. You are not doing it for recognition and praise; you are doing it for personal satisfaction.

My daddy taught me, "Any job worth doing is a job worth doing right."

Even if no one notices what you do, do it right. You will know, and you will feel good knowing that you did it perfectly!

Do it right.

You Can Never
Know It All

All of us cherish those friendships we have with people who have had a major impact on our lives.

One of my friends saved my life. Can I prove that? No. But I believe he did. That's enough for me. I believed I was dying and he said I was. Since, in my opinion, he was the smartest man I ever knew, I believed him.

Dr. Anthony A. Malizia, Jr., a nationally known urologist, was my friend and my physician. Tony had read all fifty-one volumes of the Harvard Classics, and he remembered what he read. He had a memory that was photographic.

When I visited him, he provided outstanding health care as well as an intellectually stimulating discussion of almost any subject you can imagine. With that background information, you can join me in recognizing the impact of this statement.

He started our conversation that day by saying, "The greatest enemy of learning is knowing."

Tony Malizia knew more than any man I have known, yet he was well aware that he didn't know it all. He had that proper balance of confidence and humility that made him a great doctor.

Think about how this applies to you, to me, and to those with whom we work.

To begin, we must clearly understand what we do and don't know. There will never be a situation in which we will know everything before we act. We must realize that all decisions are based on partial information. That means there will always be some degree of risk. A decision may be good or bad, an action may work or it may not. We must . . . take risks.

When that time comes, two people are doomed to failure: the know-it-all and the person who says, "I need more information." Neither is worthy of responsibility.

The risk of the know-it-all is easily recognized. No one trusts a know-it-all.

At the same time, the person who claims he or she needs more information is often erroneously considered to be wise, when in reality he or she is simply afraid to act.

When it is time to act, we all need to recognize that no matter how much or what we know, we don't know it all. Since we can never know it all, we must be prepared to act with the best partial information available, within a reasonable period of time. A person paralyzed by the fear of not knowing everything is doomed to failure.

We must learn to trust our judgment and to act! The confidence of your fellow workers will depend on how well you balance the incomplete information with the time risk.

They will trust you when they see that you have the confidence to make a decision on a timely basis and the humility to gather enough information, and that you then act without being afraid.

Confident humility will make it possible to gain the trust and support of your fellow workers, so you must not be afraid to act.

Take risks.

Prove that you are qualified for responsibility.

Take Responsibility

There was a time when I was in the war.

No, I am not referring to the wars in Vietnam, Iraq, or Afghanistan. I was in the career war!

Surely, you know the war—you are very likely in that war now. It is the war in which everyone is fighting for titles, authority, rewards, and recognition. You don't receive medals for recognition of your performance; instead, you get a new title for your nameplate, the key to the executive rest room, reserved parking, or a corner office.

All around me, everyone was competing with everyone else. None of my coworkers wanted to work with me, and I didn't want to work with them, either.

I was not about to permit another person to profit from my efforts. Why should I share my success with those who were trying to beat me to the next promotion? If there was to be recognition for successful achievements, I wanted it—and I knew they wanted it too. None of us wanted to share credit for anything we accomplished.

Everyone wanted to do the low-risk, easy, "sure thing" assignments. With those tasks, we could always look like a winner and receive public recognition for a job well done.

Of course, there was a lot of competition for those assignments; every person was available and ready for action! That was the positive side of the war.

Yes, the fight on that side was serious and intense, but it was nothing compared to the negative side. It was amazing how the competition would simply disappear when a tough or a difficult and dirty assignment was about to be announced. If there was the slightest possibility of failure, no one wanted that job, because failure might create doubts about one's competence. Responsibility must always be avoided. There was no point in risking one's career with a failure. No one wanted that!

Does this sound familiar to you? Are you in that war too?

One day I realized that this is no way to manage a career.

I had been seeking authority and titles; as a result, no one wanted to work with me, because we were competing with each other.

I decided that, from that day forward, rather than seeking authority, I would simply . . .

Take responsibility.

The results were amazing!

When I took responsibility, especially for the difficult and dirty assignments, I no longer had a problem getting coworkers to join with me. They knew that Jimmy was taking responsibility. If anything went wrong, if there was a failure, I would take the blame. If the results were positive, however, they would share in the recognition.

My coworkers learned that when I took responsibility for the worst assignments—you know the kind, with impossible completion dates, customers who cannot be satisfied, unrealistic budgets, the difficult and dirty—and then we successfully completed them, that there was plenty of recognition for all of us to share. They could share the recognition without risk of being responsible for failure.

Then, rather than competition, I had cooperation. Together, our results soared to new heights. I had implemented one of the most powerful principles of Creative Followership:

Take responsibility.

When I decided to stop seeking authority and to start taking responsibility, I discovered that there was no limit to what I could accomplish!

Dealing with Professional Discouragement

Discouragement is a challenge for every executive. Actually, discouragement is a challenge for every one of us, no matter what our role, in our personal lives and in our professional lives.

As a teenager, I realized that I could face discouragement without fear. I learned that I had control of my reaction to discouragement and that if I put up a good fight, I would win.

My fighting method was to constantly remind myself, *I am not easily discouraged.* It was amazing how that helped me through difficult times.

Later, I learned that what worked in my personal life also worked in my professional life.

It worked so well that I made it one of my principles of Creative Followership.

Do not be easily discouraged.

For example, it would have been easy to become discouraged in 1971, as we were working to expand Chick-fil-A. By the end of 1970, we had seven Chick-fil-A restaurants in shopping malls—three in Georgia, two in North Carolina, one in South Carolina, and one in Texas.

Not many for three years of effort.

Even though enclosed malls were opening at an increasing rate all over the country, we were having great difficulty getting locations. The malls wanted tearooms, coffee shops, and fine dining. In addition, most of the major mall developers wanted only tenants with AAA credit ratings, which Chick-fil-A did not have.

Chick-fil-A offered quick, high-volume service, but the response of the developers was "We are not interested." I had heard that before, many times, but I am not easily discouraged.

When we learned that the Rouse Company, one of the premier mall developers, was to open a new mall in Atlanta in the summer of 1971, we went after a location. Off I went to their offices in Maryland, armed with determination and enthusiasm. Unfortunately, they did not want what they thought of as a fried chicken restaurant in one of their classy malls.

I made so many trips to their office that when I arrived the receptionist would announce, "Chicken Little is here again." They were courteous but firm in their reply: "We are not interested." But I am not easily discouraged.

Then, when we learned that the leasing agents were visiting the construction site, Truett Cathy and I took Chick-fil-A food to them. Still they said, "We are not interested."

That is when I started a postcard deluge.

We had picture postcards of Chick-fil-A sandwiches and

Postcards to the Rouse Company

the Oglethorpe Mall restaurant in Savannah, Georgia. Each day, every day, I sent a postcard to the vice president of leasing. Typical messages were "Only Chick-fil-A serves America's favorite main dish as a sandwich!," "At Chick-fil-A in Greenbriar Mall, 1970 sales equaled $626.32 per square foot, without opening on Sunday!," "At Chick-fil-A, service

IS instantaneous!," and "At Chick-fil-A, we have no bones to sell, only chicken!"

After several weeks, I received a telephone call: "Stop the cards; we will make a deal."

If I were easily discouraged, we would not have gotten the location in Perimeter Mall—a restaurant that has been one of Chick-fil-A's top performing mall locations for more than forty years. Not only that, but making the deal to locate in Perimeter Mall opened doors with many other developers, and it established for us a mutually beneficial, ongoing relationship with the Rouse Company.

The losses that people experience when they are easily discouraged are immeasurable. On the other hand, the gains from overcoming discouragement may be difficult to measure, but they are major contributors to our success and satisfaction.

I recommend that you work to develop this same attitude.

Do not be easily discouraged.

Are you willing to try it?

Do Not Hoard Authority

A creative follower is constantly looking for opportunities to do what the boss does not like to do, and then he or she does those things better than they have ever been done before.

By this process, you add value to the boss by giving him or her more time to do what the boss likes to do, and probably does best. And, of course, it also makes you more valuable to the boss.

You may be thinking, "That process could not go on forever. There are only so many hours in the day. I cannot do all of my work plus all the things the boss does not like to do, as well."

First, let me assure you that there is no need to worry about your plate becoming too full to handle. Once you begin to gain authority through Creative Followership, you will discover others who would like to pick up some of the pieces of your work.

Never fall for the temptation to hoard your tasks. The only way you can add to your plate is if others remove something from your plate. I found that other people were coming and gladly taking pieces of my job away.

Do not hoard authority.

This principle is one that far too many people are not willing to practice, because they are not secure enough in their own abilities to continue the process into the future. Territorialism is something that not only wastes resources and kills the spirit of cooperation but also holds the hoarding individuals back and prevents their own growth and advancement. I loved my work; it was always changing. And that is another key to enjoyment and satisfaction in your career. Let capable people take pieces away; do not mark off territory.

Because I did enjoy my work, other people thought they might like to do what I did. I did not mind seeing others take things away from me, especially if it was a task I did not enjoy doing. Some of those tasks I really liked to do, but I let someone with more time, and in certain instances greater ability, have that specific task.

This synergism of tasks evolving and revolving is a good thing for everyone, and it is extremely healthy for the organization. The process of movement and dynamic change or constant motion is a positive for growth and innovation. We can grow and evolve as individuals when we get new responsibilities and when old responsibilities become new tasks in someone else's hands. It is never good to have people in the organization who get tasks or responsibilities and then hang on to them at all costs.

Some people feel threatened by anyone who has taken a piece of their job away. Instead of recognizing an opportunity to move on to new and more challenging tasks and potentially more authority, they do whatever is necessary to repossess a task, defending their perceived territory.

Territorialism is poisonous to productivity and benefits no one—especially the fence owner. Avoid territorialism! Learn to see beyond what you think and feel is your plot of land and learn to look up to the horizon and see the vast uncharted territory of new opportunity.

Do not hoard authority.

If you want to move forward, then something you do now has to go to make room for the new.

Make Your Boss Look Good

Of all the Creative Followership principles, Principle 6: Make Your Boss Look Good is the most difficult for many people to accept.

However, when it is understood, it is not at all difficult to practice.

To start, I want to emphasize that the creative follower should always practice this principle.

Make your boss look good.

As you begin to practice the Creative Followership principles, you will see many ways to make your boss look good. Don't hesitate! Do it!

How do you make your boss look good?

You make your boss look good by implementing Creative Followership Principle 3: Do What Your Boss Does Not Like to Do and Principle 4: Do What Your Boss Does Not Do Well.

Keep working to make your boss look good and to help your boss advance in the organization. Your boss will protect you and provide you with the materials and resources that you need to keep supporting him or her.

In the event that you have a boss who is not smart

enough to see that you are helping him to accomplish his tasks, remember Principle 1: Choose Your Boss! You are a volunteer.

Yes, even if you are not happy with the boss you work for now, make that boss look good.

You gain nothing when you try to make someone else look bad. You cannot make yourself look good by trying to make another person look bad. Trying to make others look bad will cost you the support of your coworkers and possibly your job. Forget bad-mouthing.

Do your best to make your boss look good, even if you are actively engaged in the process of choosing a new boss. You will want an excellent reference.

If you are seeking a new boss within your organization, those with authority over your boss are probably very familiar with your boss's strengths and weaknesses. If your boss has a sudden surge in talent or a brand-new skill set the people in charge have never seen before, they will notice the change. It is very likely they also will recognize the true source of talent, and your actions will stand out against the background of what your boss did in the past.

But avoid any temptation to help the process of discovery along. Think about the risk of undermining and competing with the boss. These things get one fired, not promoted.

If you are seeking a position with another organization, don't forget that it is easier to get a job when you have a job. Doing the best you can and maintaining a standard of excellent performance is the wisest route to keeping yourself employed. And while you are still there, remember to learn all you can!

Make your boss look good.

After all that has been said, you know that I am not advocating mindless acceptance of all that the boss says and does. For example, if you believe the boss has made a poor decision, share your point of view, then accept and support the outcome—barring anything illegal, immoral, or in violation of policy. You should of course not be working for someone whose actions contradict good moral judgment.

Any Job Worth Doing

My daddy, Horace S. Collins, planted a large garden in our backyard.

No, let me correct that. My daddy turned our backyard into a garden.

During World War II, most of the folks in our neighborhood planted a "victory garden." It was the patriotic thing to do, and for our large family, it was the economical thing to do.

No other neighbors turned their entire large backyard into a garden. They all left a major portion of the yard for their children to play. But Daddy was a farmer at heart. He loved to plant seeds and see them sprout and grow. He grew so much that my mother canned vegetables in the summer for us to eat the following winter. He was a good and productive farmer.

My younger brothers and I were assigned the task of taking care of that large garden. I hated the job, especially the weeding. It was our toughest responsibility. Weeds grew so fast that we could never get ahead. They sprouted out of nowhere overnight and multiplied faster than rabbits.

My daddy had unreasonably high expectations of his

boys. He expected perfection.

Every day, when he came home from work, he inspected that large garden. If he found a single sprig of green weed, he would have us do the weeding over again, saying, "Any job worth doing is worth doing right."

I hated those weeds. I hated the garden. I hated the discipline.

It took time for me to appreciate the lesson my daddy taught me. Later, I would treasure the lesson and the memory of him saying, "Any job worth doing is worth doing right."

My daddy had taught me, at an early age, one of the principles of Creative Followership:

Do it right.

As I grew older, I was dismayed by the number of people I encountered who either did not know or chose to disregard this principle.

Often, they semi-apologized and excused themselves with statements such as "Nobody will know the difference" or "I'm not paid enough to worry about getting it perfect" or "My boss does not appreciate me. Why should I care?" And, of course, there is the classic statement "This is close enough for government work."

If I left a task poorly executed, I would know, and I would not be able to forget that I did not do my best. I knew that if I wanted the boss to increase my pay, I had to convince him that my work was so well done that he had to pay me more or someone else would. I knew the best way to earn my boss's appreciation was to exceed his expectations.

When I finish each day, I want to reflect on what I have done and be able to honestly say, "I did my best today."

Surely, you also want to say, "I did my best today."

Do it right.

My Most Demanding Boss

As soon as I learned that we had a problem at Chick-fil-A, the first thing I did was to work out a suitable solution. The second thing I did was inform Truett Cathy about the problem—and about the solution that was already under way.

My boss said that he didn't like problems. That was only partly true. Truett enjoyed solving the problems of his choice. He tackled some huge and difficult problems, but he liked to choose his problems.

Like every boss, he enjoyed those days when the only big news was that sales were increasing and customer satisfaction was soaring. That brought a smile to his face and comfort to all of his followers.

One day, I went into the boss's office to brief him on a problem and to explain the remedy that I had already implemented. Truett seemed satisfied with the action that had been taken.

As I turned to leave, I said, "Truett, you don't need to worry about these problems. I'll take care of them. That's what you are paying me to do."

"Oh, no!" he said. "I am paying you to *prevent* problems."

I immediately stopped, stunned, struck with reality of the high level of his expectations and his trust in me.

Truett Cathy was my best boss, and my most demanding boss.

Prevent problems? That was his expectation!

He had confidence in my determination to meet his expectations.

Actually, he knew that I would do more than he expected, and he wanted to clearly communicate his expectation.

Do more than is expected.

As a youngster working part time, I had learned that to earn more money I had to make myself more valuable. At that time, making money was my main objective.

Right away, it was obvious that just meeting the boss's minimum expectations would never get me where I wanted to go. I had to do more, and do it better than my coworkers. If I wanted to become more valuable, I needed to take on additional responsibility and do more than was expected.

I did, and it worked.

Many years later, when I went to work for Truett, I had honed my do-more-than-expected approach to a sharp-edged career advancement tool. I used it from day one. I was "all-in" and totally committed.

My commitment to not just meeting but also exceeding Truett's expectations earned me his unwavering support. He trusted me to do whatever was needed, even when he had no idea whether I knew how to do it or not.

He knew that I would let nothing stop me from success-fully completing whatever we set out to do, no matter how difficult the task.

Do you want that kind of support from your boss?

Try raising your performance bar from problem solver to problem preventer.

Do more than is expected.

It worked for me.

It will work for you.

The Advantage
of Not Knowing

I am glad I did not know. I am glad no one knew.
When I went to work for Truett Cathy to help him
build the Chick-fil-A restaurant chain, I was the third staff
employee. None of us knew. None of us had built, operated, or even worked in a restaurant chain. No one had
any experience in organizing a franchise system.

We did not know how to do it, and that was an advantage!

If we had started with experience from another restaurant chain, today's Chick-fil-A probably would be like one
of the other chicken chains, or maybe like one of the hamburger chains. It is even more likely that we would have
failed, like so many other restaurant chains that are now
long gone and forgotten.

Because we did not know, we were free to invent and
create a restaurant chain that was different from anything
else in the industry.

I am glad I did not know.

I am glad no one knew.

As you'll recall, my friend Dr. Malizia told me that "the
greatest enemy of learning is knowing."

Think about that. When we are confident that we know something, we close our mind to ideas, suggestions, thoughts, and points of view that are not consistent with what we know. Imagination, creativity, and questioning cease to penetrate the ruling confidence of experience that is in control of our minds. The adventure of exploration and discovery are choked off by the pride of knowing "I have been there and done that."

That's when we lose the advantage of not knowing!

Remember when your organization hired an outsider from another organization, similar to yours? Remember how people sought that person's knowledge, asking, "How did you do it at . . . ?" Remember how everyone listened with a quiet reverence to the wise tales of wonderful results? Remember how the new person relished the attention?

Is it any wonder that he or she was so free in sharing that valuable knowledge? He or she believed, "I have been hired to help this organization become like the one I left." As a result, didn't your organization become more like the one that person had left?

I am glad that the top-level management at Chick-fil-A had never worked for another restaurant chain. I am glad Chick-fil-A is not like any other restaurant chain. I am glad that we did not lose . . .

The advantage of not knowing.

I am glad I did not know.

I am glad no one knew.

Always Do Your Best

I did not like school. I liked to learn, but I did not like school.

Most of the time, I was bored and disinterested. My body was present in the classroom but my mind was far away.

I liked learning what I considered useful and practical, so I found subjects like math and mechanical drawing interesting. Until I entered Georgia Tech, I was confident that I would be the next Frank Lloyd Wright. Why should an architect be bothered with English, social studies, and that sort of material?

In addition to being disinterested, I also thought the teaching methods were too rigid and required too much rote memorization, rather than creative thinking. As a result of my attitude, I did not earn good grades.

I did not like school.

However, when I entered the eighth grade I encountered a subject that I loved: algebra! It made sense to me. It was practical. I had no trouble understanding it.

For algebra, I was "all-in"!

During the first quarter, on every test, I received a perfect grade, 100 percent. On every classroom assignment and every homework assignment, my grade was 100 percent. I imagined taking my report card home at the end of the first quarter and showing my parents a perfect score, 100 percent!

To my disbelief, the grade on my report card was 99 percent. When I confronted my teacher, she said, "No one is perfect." I was totally disappointed and discouraged.

During the next quarter, I put forth no effort and received a grade of 71 percent—and a lecture from my teacher.

"James, you didn't even try," she said. "You must always do your best."

I decided to do my best for the third quarter, and again I received perfect grades of 100 percent on everything. Yet, at the end of the third quarter, when I looked at my report card, I had again received only a 99 percent.

I was angry. Again I confronted the teacher, and again she said, "No one is perfect."

During the fourth quarter, I did just enough to get by. If I couldn't get the recognition I deserved, I didn't care what the grade was, as long as I passed the course.

When the teacher passed out the grades for the fourth quarter, she called me to her desk. She handed me my quarterly report, with its grade of 79 percent, and proceeded to give me advice.

"James, if you ever want to amount to anything, you must always do your best."

Mrs. Kathleen Dolphin taught me more than basic algebra; she embedded an important lesson in the mind of

FULTON COUNTY HIGH SCHOOLS
REPORT OF

Collins, James   B-6

STUDENT'S LAST NAME   FIRST NAME AND INITIAL   HOME CLASS

SCHOOL YEAR 1950 1951

SUBJECTS	1ST QTR.	2ND QTR.	3RD QTR.	4TH QTR.	UNIT	SUBJECTS	1ST QTR.	2ND QTR.	3RD QTR.	4TH QTR.	UNIT
DAYS ABSENT		11	2	6		APPLIED SCIENCE					
TIMES TARDY		3				NATURAL SCIENCE					
CONDUCT	100	94	100	95		AGRICULTURE					
ENGLISH 1-2	85	83	77	85	1	BOOKKEEPING					
PUB. SPEAKING						STENOGRAPHY					
JOURNALISM						TYPEWRITING					
RADIO W'KSHOP						OFFICE PRACTICE					
LATIN						COM'L LAW					
FRENCH						SALESMANSHIP					
SPANISH						BUSINESS TR.					
INTERCULTURAL RELATIONS						BUSINESS ARITH.					
HISTORY						HOME ECONOMICS					
WORLD GEOG. & VOCA. GUIDANCE	85	73	82	64	1	FAMILY RELATIONS					
ECONOMICS						HEALTH SCIENCE					
PROBLEMS IN DEMOCRACY						8TH GR. IND. ARTS					
GOVERNMENT						MECH. DRAWING	95	95	95	95	1
ECONOMIC GEOGRAPHY						WOOD SHOP					
ARITHMETIC						METAL SHOP					
ALGEBRA I-II	99	71	99	79	1	ELECTRIC SHOP					
GEOMETRY						ART					
TRIGONOMETRY						MUSIC					
GEN'L SCIENCE						MILITARY	77	83	91	77	½
BIOLOGY						PHYSICAL ED					
PHYSICS						RELATED STUDIES					
CHEMISTRY						DE OR DCT WORK					

Parents are invited and urged to cooperate in every way with the teacher.
Passing grade is 70

Signature of Parent
1st Quar. *M. S. Collins*
2nd Quar. *H. S. Collins*
3rd Quar. *M. S. Collins*
FORM 30 (REV.)

Mrs. Lucy Lowe
Signature of Teacher
Russell

HIGH SCHOOL

Jimmy's Report Card for 1950-1951

a cocky, rebellious, and uncooperative teenager. It is a lesson that I have never forgotten.

I learned that it didn't matter who kept the score or whether they kept it correctly. It didn't matter whether I got credit or recognition. What mattered was that I *knew* I had done my best.

I didn't like Mrs. Dolphin's method, but I treasure her lesson.

Always do your best.

For almost sixty-four years, I have heard her speak to me. Thousands of times I have heard her voice, and I still hear it today. I did want to amount to something, and I slowly learned to follow her advice.

When I retired, I was asked, "If you could do it over again, what would you change about your career?"

My reply: "Nothing. I always did my best."

Always do your best.

Preach Your Own Sermon

I was looking forward to John's sermon.

John (not his real name) was a loved and respected associate minister at our church. He didn't often have an opportunity to preach, but when he did, he very effectively delivered a message, which was further validated because he was a model husband, father, and friend to all.

As soon as John began speaking on this particular day, though, I knew something was wrong.

His opening illustration was not like those he typically used. It was not his, and I had heard it word for word very recently.

Not only had I heard the opening illustration; I had heard the entire sermon!

At that time, I subscribed to cassette tapes offered by several well-known preachers, as well as motivational tapes and books on tape. (Those were the days before CDs.) Even today, I always keep a good supply of recordings in my car, and I listen to them while driving.

For twenty-five minutes on that particular day, John delivered the exact sermon that I had heard on a cassette tape just a few weeks earlier.

When I returned home after the church service, I put into my tape player a sermon from Bob Russell of Southeast Christian Church in Louisville, Kentucky.

Yes, it was the same sermon, same illustrations.

I was disappointed and concerned for John. It was not John's sermon. Most likely, I was the only person who heard that sermon and knew what had happened. Even so, I was not the most important person who knew. John knew.

John is my friend. Monday, I went to visit with him.

I didn't go to criticize him for what he had done but to encourage him to do what he should have done—to be himself.

I reminded John that we loved and respected him not for what he preached but for his sincerity, because he practiced what he preached. When he used another man's sermon, John undermined and denied us his sincerity and the truth that meant so much to us. His integrity was at stake.

I encouraged him to preach his own sermons and to continue to show us the real John, the John we loved and respected.

How about you? Are you preaching your own sermon? Are you living the real you, or are you trying to imitate someone else? There will always be someone present who knows that it is not the real you. Certainly, you will know.

Be yourself.

When I was young, I tried to imitate people I admired. It did not work. I had to learn to forget about imitating other people. I had to learn that I could only be successful at being myself.

Finally, I realized that I cannot live with a fake me!

Can you live with a fake you?

Be yourself.

The Man Nobody Knows

Over the years, I have heard people say, "When I think of what Jesus did for me, it brings tears to my eyes." It never affected me that way!

For me, accepting Jesus was an intellectual decision. There was nothing emotional about it. I have never considered myself an emotional person. As a youngster, I learned about the claims of Christ. They made sense to me. I believed them, accepted them, and was baptized.

Then, about fifty years ago, I entered a used bookstore. I found an old book there with an interesting title, *The Man Nobody Knows*. The title caught my attention, but it was the author's name that motivated me to examine the book more closely. I knew Bruce Barton's reputation as a very successful businessman. He was a pioneer in modern advertising, one of the founders of the Batten, Barton, Durstine and Osborne advertising agency, and a former U.S. congressman. Bruce Barton was a man I respected.

Barton's book was a businessman's view of Jesus. I wanted to read it.

This book had a major impact on my life! I read it at a

crucial time, a time of extreme intellectual and spiritual struggle.

Especially significant to me was the way Barton painted his word picture of Jesus coming to the end of His life. Jesus is nailed to the cross, dying. He has been abandoned by the crowds, run out of His hometown, shunned by His family, and deserted by His disciples—even betrayed by one of them.

Jesus is dying. It looks like His enemies have won and it is all over.

Then the gloomy silence is broken by a voice.

"Jesus." It is one of the criminals on the cross next to Him. "Jesus," he calls, "remember me when You come into Your kingdom" (Luke 23:42).

As I read that, I thought, *What power of presence! What strength of spirit!*

This criminal believed that Jesus, even though He was dying on a cross, could save him!

For the first time, tears did flow, because I realized who Jesus is, what He had done, and for whom He had done it. He had done it for me!

That experience changed my life!

It changed my attitude. It changed my motives. It created in me a thankful heart. I wanted to give and to serve!

Since that day, I have read *The Man Nobody Knows* every year. I have given copies to hundreds of people and have recommended it to thousands.

I recommend *The Man Nobody Knows* to you!

Do the Dirty
and Difficult Jobs

I was on a mission of encouragement.

Matt Wilson was discouraged. His field consultant had told me that he was *very* discouraged.

Matt was a talented young man who had shown a lot of promise working in one of our restaurants. The Operator he worked for had recommended him for the interim manager program, because he considered Matt a good candidate to become a franchisee.

The interim managers provided temporary management for restaurants when the departure and arrival dates of franchisee changes did not match. Usually, the restaurants were in good condition and didn't need much more than a temporary figurehead on the premises for a short time.

Occasionally, however, an interim manager found him- or herself in a very difficult situation, one in which sales were declining, customers were not being satisfied, employees were discouraged, and maintenance had been neglected.

Matt was in one of those difficult situations.

When I arrived at the restaurant, Matt immediately made it clear to me how discouraged he was. He was disappointed that he had been given such a mess to straighten out. He spent a long time telling me all that was wrong.

He had expected to be assigned to a well-run unit without problems, an assignment that he could easily handle and that would make him look good. His major concern was to build positive impressions so that he could to get a franchise of his own.

Unfortunately, he did not realize what a wonderful opportunity he had to show how good he was by taking on a dirty and difficult task.

I advised Matt that if he wanted to demonstrate how good he was, he should employ the following principle of Creative Followership:

Do the dirty and difficult jobs.

"When you attack and conquer the dirty and difficult tasks," I told him, "you can be a hero. You turn around a declining, deteriorating situation and you receive recognition and reward.

"In fact," I added, "it is much easier to look good when you tackle dirty and difficult tasks. If you go into a restaurant that is already a top-rated performer, you are much more likely to mess up the situation and make it worse. What do you think that would say about your performance?"

Do you want to make a difference?

Do you want to demonstrate your ability and effectiveness?

Do you want reward and recognition?

Do the dirty and difficult jobs.

Matt is the bright and capable guy that his boss had recommended. Once he adjusted his viewpoint, he recognized the opportunity and put that restaurant in order, satisfied customers, created a happy work environment for the employees, and increased sales.

He added a victory to his résumé!

Are you as smart as Matt? Then follow his example.

Do the dirty and difficult jobs.

Who Is Going to Fix It?

My coauthor, Michael Cooley, and I were on our way to a speaking engagement about a five-hour drive from home, where we would be making videos for group study of the principles of Creative Followership.

Along the way, we decided to stop at one of our favorite hamburger chain restaurants. I remember how much I liked the burgers, fries, and milkshakes the first time I tasted them, on a trip to Florida in the 1950s. Sixty years later, the food still tastes the same. I like it!

After eating, when I went into the men's restroom, I was disappointed to see that the commode would not flush. The handle was obviously disconnected inside the water tank.

I intended to tell the manager, but I gave up that plan because I was in a hurry, the restaurant was very busy, and I could not spot anyone who seemed to be the person in charge. I knew that every one of the male employees would go into that restroom at some point, and that someone would check the status of the supplies, and that at some time, at least once, the restrooms would be cleaned for the day.

Someone would see that the problem was fixed.

The next day, on our way home, we stopped again at the same restaurant. (Did I mention that I like the food?) The restaurant was even busier than it had been the day before.

Before leaving, I went into the men's restroom.

I could not believe what I found! That commode flusher had not been fixed!

How many people knew that it needed it fixing? At least every male employee of that restaurant on duty during the previous twenty-four hours must have known it needed fixing. Why didn't they do something about it? The managers that had been there during the previous twenty-four hours should have known. Did no one tell the female managers? How about the male managers? Someone should have made sure that the manager on duty knew!

Who was going to fix it? I fixed it!

Because the flush handle was obviously disconnected from the flapper, the connection must be broken. I lifted the porcelain lid from the water tank at the back of the commode and immediately saw that the chain connecting the flapper with the handle lever was unhooked. I hooked the chain back in place, flushed the commode, and replaced the lid. It took me less than one minute!

Then I went to find the manager. After I asked three different employees to get the manager, and waited several minutes, the manager on duty finally arrived. I gave a brief summary of why I knew that the problem had existed for more than twenty-four hours, and stated that I had finally fixed the simple problem myself (something that any 12-year-old could have done).

The reply I received was, "I didn't know about it."

I said, "You should have known. The situation has existed for more than twenty-four hours!"

Do you know why the manager didn't know? I know why.

No one had taken any initiative to solve the simple problem, for more than twenty-four hours! No one took responsibility! There were no mustangs working there!

Far too many workplaces discourage initiative. Instead, the emphasis is on following the rules. Thus, the people I call mustangs won't work there. Mustangs get reprimanded for taking initiative and doing things without prior approval, or that are in variance to the standard rules. Only the mules—employees that need continuous prodding, pushing, and kicking—will stay with such an organization.

Would you want to work there? I wouldn't work there!

Mustangs take responsibility and make things happen, and they often ignore the rules. They can be difficult to handle, and sometimes they must be restrained, but they get things done.

A mustang does not ask, "Who is going to fix it?" A mustang assigns someone to do it, calls a service person, tells the boss what needs to be done, or does it him- or herself and reports later that it has been done.

With whom would you rather work?

I love to work with mustangs!

It is better to restrain mustangs than kick mules.

If you are a boss thinking of training employees to take the initiative or to be mustangs, forget it. You can't teach initiative; you must recruit it.

And if you want to keep mustangs, remember that a little restraint is okay, but we mustangs will not stay inside a fence.

How Will You Keep
the Impossible Deadline?

It did not seem like an impossible deadline when I promised to open that restaurant at 10:00 a.m. on August 12, 1971. After all, we had opened ten other restaurants, all of them on time, and we at Chick-fil-A were serious about our promises.

We had promised to open four new restaurants in 1971. All of them were to open on a specific date coinciding with the grand opening of a new shopping mall.

We didn't make the commitments based on whether it would be easy or hard to keep our promises. We didn't make the promises based on any ifs, ands, or buts. We simply promised to open the restaurants on time, and we did.

The first opening of 1971 was relatively easy. The next two were really tough. The fourth, in Cordova Mall, Pensacola, Florida, was a nightmare come true!

Early in life, I had learned to think of the hard and challenging times as character-building opportunities. The year 1971 was an unforgettable character-building opportunity.

The restaurant in Cordova Mall was to be our eleventh Chick-fil-A restaurant in a shopping center. With the assistance of our newest staff member, Perry Ragsdale, I had drawn all of the construction plans. However, to get our building permit in Pensacola, the plans would have to be redrawn by an architect registered in Florida. We also would not be able to build out the leasehold improvements ourselves, as we usually did. Instead, it was necessary to hire a locally licensed contractor. That would be tough, because there was a critical shortage of local contractors interested in building out a restaurant in the new mall. Finally, licenses and permits were unbelievably hard to secure, compared to what we had experienced in other locations.

There were eighty-five store locations in Cordova Mall, and most of the merchants intended to open on time: August 12.

Unfortunately, construction of the mall itself was far behind schedule. Usually, a mall would be completed well in advance of the time individual stores started to build out their own leasehold improvements. Having the mall under construction while the stores were trying to finish and furnish their stores created a living nightmare.

After finally securing a local general contractor and getting all of our permits and licenses, it became apparent to me that we were facing an impossible task in getting the restaurant open on time. However, I had promised the mall developer, the landlord, my boss, and myself that we would open on time. Could I keep the impossible deadline?

To keep that promise, I decided to move my family to a motel on the beach and to spend all day, every day, on the site until that restaurant was open and operating. I was committed to opening on time, but I knew that I couldn't do it alone.

Before we left home, I had a sign painted on a large piece of white vinyl wall covering, to hang in the mall above the front of the restaurant and confirm my promise. The sign read, "YES! Chick-fil-A will open Aug. 12!" I expected the sign would encourage people to take me seriously and would motivate them to help me open on time.

The response was just the opposite! The people working in the mall and the other stores thought it was funny. They laughed, joked, and made fun of the sign. They continually reminded me that it would never happen, that I had set myself an impossible deadline.

The situation started bad and got worse. Every day it seemed that I was further behind than the day before. It was summer and awfully hot inside the mall because the air-conditioning for the mall itself was not yet finished. I stayed there all day, every day, persuading subcontractors and individual workers to come work on the Chick-fil-A restaurant in the evening, when they finished working on their regular jobs. I tried to make friends with every worker.

Workers in the mall joked and continued to tell me it would never happen. After a while, they had almost convinced me that it *was* an impossible deadline. I began to hate that sign.

Personal problems developed. My hair started falling out in small patches. The dermatologist said this was caused by stress and that the hair would grow back, but

Two days before opening Cordova Mall

that the patches would probably be white. Oh, no! An acquaintance of mine had had that problem. When his hair grew back, he looked like a black leopard with white spots.

I was tired and weary. Why not just give up, like so many other merchants were doing? I couldn't. My promise was on that sign.

Every morning, all the way from the motel to the mall, I prayed, but each day it seemed that we were further behind than the day before. I found myself praying all day, every day, but I could not see an answer. Each day the situation was worse than the day before.

Every day someone else made another joke about the sign. I hated that sign.

Even the local newspaper thought we had set an impossible deadline. Two days before we were to open, the *Pensacola News* took a photograph of the front of our unfinished restaurant, which it published the day before the mall was to open. The floor tile had not been laid, the air-conditioning was not in, the ceiling was not in place, and the restaurant equipment had not been installed. The caption read, "SIGN ATTESTS CHICK-FIL-A WILL BE IN BUSINESS . . . although much work appears necessary before doors open."

I hated that sign! Without that sign, I could have found an excuse. Once I put that sign up where anyone and everyone could see it, though, there was no way I could back out on my commitment.

On August 12, at 3:00 a.m., the night before we were to open, we went to the motel for a three-hour break to take a bath, freshen up, and be back at 6:00 a.m. to open at 10:00 a.m.

When we arrived at 6:00 a.m., grand opening day, the air-conditioning workers were still installing the ductwork and some of the restaurant equipment was not yet installed.

We had two cash registers. When I plugged them in, one caught on fire! I had to borrow a cash register from a hot dog restaurant that was not going the make the opening.

Amazingly, at 10:00 a.m., August 12, Chick-fil-A opened in Cordova Mall!

We were one of only eighteen of the eighty-five stores to open on time. How had we kept the impossible deadline?

The mall manager came by and said, "Collins, get that sign down!" He had never wanted me to put it up, but he had finally agreed to let me keep the sign up until opening day.

I climbed the ladder and reached out to take down the sign. As I touched it, a surge of energy rippled through my body, and I recalled Isaiah 65:24: *Before they call I will answer.*

God had answered my prayers before I ever left Atlanta!

Do Executives
Really Retire?

D o executives really ever retire?
Too many executives enjoy their retirement cele-
bration but don't get out of the business.

You know this is how it often happens, because you have
seen it. Some executives want to hang on in a consulting role.
Others are still anxious to share their wisdom and advice
with those young people who assumed their responsibilities.
Their heart is still in the business, even though the information bank in their mind is outdated almost overnight.

When I retired, I was determined that I would avoid
the kind of the mistake made by my friend Walt.

Walt had recently retired from a Fortune 500 corporation. He had been the senior officer responsible for his
corporation's direct customer services. One evening, Walt
received a telephone call from a close friend, whom he had
known for decades, telling him that the caller's daughter
had been unfairly discharged from the company. Walt told
his friend that this was not the way the matter, a minor
policy violation, should have been handled, and that he
would contact his replacement about it.

Walt called the woman who had replaced him and told

her that the usual practice for that particular policy violation was to issue a reprimand and record it in the employee's personnel file, but not to dismiss the employee.

Walt's replacement listened politely until he finished, then she firmly reminded him, "Walt, you don't work here anymore."

That was Walt's last call.

Before I retired from Chick-fil-A, I made this resolution: *After I retire, I will not make any suggestions or offer any criticism.*

I never want to hear someone say, "Jimmy, you don't work here anymore."

When I retired, I retired.

Since I retired, when people ask me about the current policies, procedures, and practices of Chick-fil-A, my standard reply is, "I don't know. I am retired."

When I speak on Creative Followership, people often ask me to answer *what* and *why* questions about Chick-fil-A's actions. My reply is, "I can't discuss Chick-fil-A's strategy and tactics because I don't know anything about them. I am retired."

When I retired, I retired.

I am enjoying my retirement, because I am confident that I will never be told, "Jimmy, you don't work here anymore."

How about you? Will you really retire?

Truett Cathy, My Best Boss

S. Truett Cathy
March 14, 1921–September 8, 2014

He was my best boss.
He was my most demanding boss.
He was a leader.

Truett told me what he wanted me to do, but he did not tell me how to do it. A good boss gives direction by telling his workers what he wants them to do, and then he leaves it up to them to figure out how to do it.

He let me use my own initiative and creativity to get the job done. He was wise enough to know that if it was my creation, I was more likely to see it through, no matter how difficult the task turned out to be.

He made my role easier because he gave clear and simple instructions and did not constantly change his mind.

Truett's first instruction to me was, "I want you to help me open restaurants—and see that they *stay* open." There was definite emphasis on "*stay* open."

I knew what he wanted, and he left it to me to do whatever was necessary to get it done.

Truett Cathy and Jimmy Collins, 1993

Yes, he expected me to do it right, and "right" was to do it the way Truett liked to conduct business.

Truett expected loyalty. He wanted people to join him who were totally committed to the success of Chick-fil-A, people who would stick with him no matter how difficult the task or how long it took to complete.

Commitments made were to be kept, no matter how difficult, and no excuses were acceptable. That encouraged very careful commitment making!

All business was to be conducted with the expectation

that long-term relations would be established and maintained. He expected every person involved in Chick-fil-A's business to be a good steward of our resources and assets. He also expected that we would do business in such a manner that we would always have a positive influence on every person with whom we came in contact. Actually, he demanded it!

He never yelled at me, but he made his high expectations crystal clear.

I chose Truett as my boss.

I chose a leader worthy of my followership. I gave him my absolute loyalty, and he responded with his unwavering support.

On September 8, 2014, Truett departed this world for his eternal home. I will miss him. I am glad that while he was here, he was my boss.

Truett Cathy was my best boss.

Conclusion

This is my story.

This is my life.

My life, like yours, consists of little stories. Many of them may be buried away in the vast expanse of our memory, but they are all there, and they are our lives.

Some of those stories should be shared, need to be shared, because they can have a positive influence on other people and may help those others as they travel along on their own lifetime journey.

I have been encouraged to tell my stories. I often hear, "Tell us a story."

That is what I have shared with you: *Jimmy's Stories*.

I am pleased to share my stories with you, and I urge you to tell your stories.

Remember, we are writing our life stories as we live.

It is the little stories we create each day that make up our life stories. We have many choices, and we can write our stories to be whatever we are willing to make them.

Let's make stories that will inspire and motivate others to follow in our footsteps.

When my life story is finally complete, I want to hear

my Lord say, "Well done, good and faithful servant" (Matthew 25:21).

How do you want your story to end?

You have a choice. Make your life a great story.

Principles
—— *of* ——
Creative Followership

— 1 —
Choose Your Boss

— 2 —
Know Your Boss

— 3 —
Do What Your Boss Does Not Like to Do

— 4 —
Do What Your Boss Does Not Do Well

— 5 —
Do Not Compete with Your Boss

— 6 —
Make Your Boss Look Good

— 7 —
Take Responsibility

— 8 —
Everyone Likes Problems

— 9 —
Do Not Hoard Authority

continued on next page

continued on next page

— 32 —
Be Thankful for Strong-Willed Critics

— 33 —
Never Assume What You Can Verify

— 34 —
Use Actions and Symbols

— 35 —
Avoid Executive Privilege

Please visit

creativefollowership.com